THE MASS
IS NEVER ENDED

Rediscovering

Our Mission

to Transform

the World

Who doesn't want these three things? 1) A mission worthy of our best efforts. 2) A community that always supports us. 3) A God who continually undergirds us. In *The Mass Is Never Ended*, Greg Pierce eloquently and powerfully lays out the components of a rich, purposeful, and holy Catholic life and shows how they are—amazingly!—available to each one of us in the celebration of the Mass.

Paul Wilkes
Author of *The Seven Secrets of Successful Catholics*

There is only one Mass. . . . It is our work, Monday through Saturday. It is our worship on Sunday. Greg Pierce urges us to live the Mass all-at-once.

William Droel
Editor, *Initiatives*, National Center for the Laity

This is a beautiful, powerful book. Its simplicity and brevity can be deceiving, though. When you begin to realize that you are called to mission, and how the Mass can be celebrated from the perspective of the dismissal—for mission!—your outlook on life will be changed. Gregory Pierce has given the church a real gift in these pages!

Stephen Bevans, S.V.D.
Louis J. Luzbetak, S.V.D., Professor of Mission and Culture
Catholic Theological Union, Chicago

As a parish priest, each week I visit different parishioners at their workplace. Then I meet with them in groups of eight to ten to discuss the relationship between their faith and their work. I will never do so again without giving each one of them a copy of *The Mass Is Never Ended*.

Fr. Anthony Shonis
Associate Pastor, Henderson, Kentucky

THE MASS
IS NEVER ENDED

Rediscovering

Our Mission

to Transform

the World

Gregory F. Augustine Pierce

Author of *Spirituality at Work*

ave maria press **AmP** notre dame, indiana

> **To Abby, Nate, and Zack**
> —the work of our lives—
> may you find a mission
> worthy of your own.

Scripture quotations are from the *Contemporary English Version,* copyright © American Bible Society, 1991, 1995.

"Eucharistic Prayer" is excerpted from *Christ: The Experience of Jesus as Lord* by Edward Schillebeeckx, translated by John Bowden. Copyright © 1980. Used by permission of Crossroad Publishing.

"The Litany of Work" by David and Angela Kauffman, copyright © 1992, is used by permission of ACTA Publications.

Founded in 1865, Ave Maria Press is a ministry of the Indiana Province of Holy Cross. www.avemariapress.com

ISBN-10 1-59471-069-4   ISBN-13 978-1-59471-069-8

Cover and text design by John Carson

Printed and bound in the United States of America.

Library of Congress Cataloging-in-Publication Data

Pierce, Gregory F.
   The mass is never ended : rediscovering our mission to transform the world / Gregory F. Augustine Pierce.
      p. cm.
   ISBN-13: 978-1-59471-069-8 (pbk.)
   ISBN-10: 1-59471-069-4 (pbk.)
   1. Catholic Church--Doctrines--Popular works. 2. Christian life--Catholic authors. I. Title.

BX1754.P524 2007
248.4'82--dc22

                              2007026303

contents

....

introduction

··

MY WIFE, KATHY, and I have three young adult children, all in or college right now. Besides wanting to help them
pay for their education, Kathy and I hope for three things for
our children: We want them to be happy, holy, and fulfilled in
their lives.

To accomplish these goals, we think Abby, Nate, and Zack
need three things: a mission worthy of their lives, a community to send them forth on that mission, and a spirituality that
will allow them to be aware of the presence of God as they
attempt to carry out that mission. If they have these three
basic things, Kathy and I know they will be able to handle the
rest: the joys and sorrows, the sickness and health, the births
and deaths, the good times and the bad.

Fortunately for our kids, the Catholic Church in which they
were raised offers them all three of the things they need.

The church already offers them the most challenging and
exciting and meaningful mission that they could imagine. They
are being sent to go out into their daily lives and transform
our tired, fractured world into a place more like God would
have it.

They already belong to a community that sends them forth
on that mission through its main liturgical celebration, the

Mass. Even better, that community not only sends them forth but it also goes with them—because the mission to help bring about the kingdom of God is for everyone who claims to be a follower of Christ.

They have already been taught a spirituality that can sustain them as they carry out their mission in their daily lives on their jobs, with their families, and in their communities. That spirituality is a spirituality of work, and it is a spirituality that is especially relevant and accessible to laypeople, which is what they are.

Unfortunately, there is a problem. The problem is that our children might not realize that they already have these things. They might not recognize the God-given mission, community, and spirituality that are available to them through the church. And the problem for our children is a problem for all of us, young and old: They may not realize these great treasures of our faith because *we* do not realize them. This book, then, is a modest attempt to articulate for them and for us a spiritual path that is full, rich, and satisfying, if we but grasp it.

· · ·

Why is this book Catholic, and why is it for laypeople?

It is obviously not just Catholics who yearn for happiness, holiness, and fulfillment. Catholics are not the only ones who need mission, community, and spirituality. In fact, much of what is written here I have learned from my fellow Christians belonging to other denominations and from those of other faith traditions entirely.

Mission, community, and spirituality are basic human needs, and all people—even those who profess no religious beliefs at all—seek to fulfill them. This is so true that I have learned to speak of these matters in broad ecumenical and interfaith language, and I will continue to do so. But as a lifelong Catholic who appreciates the richness of Catholic tradition on these issues, I glory in the opportunity to address my fellow Catholics directly, using our history, language, and symbols to illuminate my points. Most of all I appreciate the opportunity to consider in depth the richness of our liturgy in supporting our mission, community, and spirituality. If others wish to peek over our shoulders or listen in on our conversation, they are welcome. But this will be a Catholic book.

. . .

My work is important to me, and your work probably is to you. It is what most of us do during most of our waking time. By work, I do not mean paid employment, although for many of us our jobs are a huge part of the work we do. By work, I mean anything that is *not* "not-work." Sleeping, for example, is not work for most of us, but I guess it could be for some. Going to the beach with little kids may be a vacation, but any of us who have done it know that there can be considerable work involved. We all know that leisure and rest and fun and hobbies are important—God thought it was so important that the Sabbath was decreed—and for the most part these activities are not work. Work is all our *other* activity, all that is *not* "not-work."

In this book, I will argue that work—at least all *good* work— includes all the activity we do to help make the world a better place, a place more like the way God would have things, what Jesus of Nazareth called the *kingdom* or the *reign* of God. I know this sounds a little pious, and most of us do not think or speak about our work like this most of the time. Nor, in truth, should we, for it would certainly put off our friends and colleagues in the workplace. When seen as the way we carry out our Christian mission, however, work takes on a much more noble status. It is no longer merely labor or toil or the daily grind. It is certainly not some kind of punishment for the sins of our forebears or an unfortunate result of the human condition. If our work—paid or unpaid, fulfilling or not, socially recognized or insignificant—is the primary way we help make the world a better place, then it is by definition important, meaningful, and holy.

Work is the way we Christians carry out a mission that is worthy of our lives because it is a mission that was given to us by the Son of God himself. While we may not always be aware of or even accept this mission, it is always there, always calling us, always able to be grasped and acted upon. And when we do act upon it, we do so by our work in the world.

Wouldn't it be wonderful if we could realize this at all times? What would the world look like if there were millions of people running around who viewed their primary purpose in life to make this world into a "New Jerusalem," a place where God's will is done "on earth as it is in heaven"? What would we be like, and how would we approach all the work we do if we were aware that we were doing God's work as we did our own work? My guess is that we would do a lot of things differently; that we would be happier, more fulfilled, and have a greater sense of accomplishment, no matter what kind of work we were doing.

• • •

But you say your work is not like that at all, or at least not very often. You say your work is difficult or meaningless or even evil at times. You quote newspaper columnist Mike Royko ("If work is so great, why do they have to pay us to do it?") or comedian Lily Tomlin ("The problem with the rat race is that even if you win, you're still a rat!").

And how about your fellow workers—your bosses, colleagues, employees, competitors? You say, *they* are certainly not trying to bring about the kingdom of God on earth! Here, too, you may be right, but you may also be exaggerating.

Maybe *some* of the people you work with are not on the same page, but maybe some of the others are just like you, waiting for someone else to be first through the door to take on this crazy mission of transforming the world. Wouldn't it be great if those of us who believed in this mission could get together once a week (or even more often, occasionally) to remind ourselves of our mission, to reflect on how we are doing, to thank and ask God for forgiveness and help, to be strengthened and trained and motivated to go back out and give it another try? Even better, wouldn't it be great if our church could design a liturgy that would accomplish all this?

The main thesis of this book is that in the Catholic Church we already have such a liturgy. It is called the Mass, which can be loosely translated as "The Sending Forth." Specifically, the Dismissal Rite at the end of Mass is supposed to send the entire congregation out into the world: "The Mass is ended. Go in peace to love and serve the Lord." This means we should carry out the mission of Jesus to proclaim and inaugurate the kingdom of God. When seen through the lens of the Dismissal, the entire Mass is aimed at this sending forth, and every single person in the congregation is being sent on a mission that is truly worthy of his or her life.

How we will carry out this mission is primarily through our work: on our jobs, with our families, and through our community and civic involvement. To accomplish this mission, we will need a spirituality that will both raise our awareness of the presence of God in our workplace and allow that awareness to inform how we will act. I call that kind of spirituality "the spirituality of work," and this book concludes with a description of that type of spirituality.

· · ·

I am a husband and father of three college-age adults. I am a writer, editor, and publisher, and I own and run a small business. I am active in civic issues and volunteer organizations. I coached kids' baseball for more than ten years and now teach high school religious education in my parish. All of this is my work, and yours is probably very much the same—if not in content, then in intensity.

Any insights in this book have been gleaned from my fifty-plus years of grappling with what it means to be a human being, a believer in a loving God, a disciple of Jesus of Nazareth, and a member of the Catholic Church. Yet these are not my thoughts alone. I believe they are the experience of a large number of followers of Christ over the centuries who have shared my sense of mission and have encountered the holy, the sacred, the divine, the transcendent, the ultimately meaningful in the midst of—not away from—the hustle and bustle of their daily lives. I have been helped by many people, especially those connected with the National Center for the Laity and my own e-mail group on faith and work, which you are invited to join at any time simply by sending me an e-mail at spiritualitywork@aol.com.

Let us go forth in peace to love and serve the Lord.

Gregory F. Augustine Pierce
Chicago, Illinois
Easter Sunday, 2007

part one
....

A Mission
Worthy of Our Lives
....

one

....

Vocation and
Mission for All

....

THERE ARE TWO words we laypeople need to redeem from misuse and misunderstanding: *vocation* and *mission*. Actually, they are yin and yang descriptions of the same reality: the call to us from God to do something with our lives, and the sending forth of us by God to do that exact thing. I realized not long ago that the vocation and mission I *have* are *not* the vocation and mission I thought I *didn't have*. Let me explain. When I was about thirteen years old, I thought I might "have a vocation." Back then, that meant I thought maybe I should become a priest. So I entered the diocesan seminary at age thirteen. At about seventeen years old, I thought I might have a mission. Back then, that meant maybe I should be a foreign missionary. So off I went to a college seminary for missionary priests.

It took me until I was about twenty-one years old to realize that I did not want to be either a priest or a missionary. Thus,

I concluded that I had neither a vocation nor a mission. Some people were called or sent, I thought, but I was not. I was fine with this decision and went out into the world to make my way.

. . .

Years later, when I was in my thirties and forties, it began to occur to me that perhaps I still did have a vocation and mission—not as a priest or missionary but to a secular profession or career. Perhaps I was being called or sent to be a community organizer, or a writer, or a publisher, or a husband, or a father—all of which I eventually became. After all, the church teaches that we are all the Body of Christ, the People of God, modern-day disciples, and that the laity have special roles to play in and to the world. Maybe my vocation/mission was as a layperson.

So I began to talk about it that way for a while, but I ran into problems. For one thing, a lot of laypeople did not like to talk about their work or their lives as a vocation or a mission. I remember learning this from a friend who is a garbage collector for the city of Chicago. He was the best garbage collector I have met: conscientious, honest, intelligent, friendly. He worked primarily to make a living and provide for his family, and when I suggested that this was some kind of mission or call from God, he actually laughed at me. He was more than willing to do his job and do it well, and he was even willing to agree that his work had social value. But he did not need to have his work "baptized" with a religious word such as *mission* or *vocation*. In fact, I think he was a little offended by the very idea.

I encountered many other people who did not view their work as a calling or mission. Sometimes people hate their jobs or their working conditions, and they cannot imagine that God wants them to do it. Others feel they are making very little contribution to the world by the particular work that they do. "I'm just an accountant (truck driver, waitress, salesperson, etc.)," they say. Or, even if they see some social value to their own work, they name plenty of other jobs that don't have any. Or people are unemployed or retired, often not by their own choosing, and it seems silly to call that a vocation or mission. All these situations seem to lead to the conclusion that some people (who have interesting, important, meaningful work) have a vocation or mission in life and other people do not, which doesn't seem right somehow.

Then there were those who tried to define vocation or mission by "state in life." Under this idea, you were called or sent to be either married (with or without children), widowed (with or without children), single (with or without children), vowed religious, or ordained. That way everybody had a vocation. The problem with this approach is that some people did not like the state of life they were in: Single people wanted to be married, married couples wanted to have kids, some religious and ordained wanted to be laicized, some laypeople wanted to be ordained. I remember commissioning a woman to write a book on the joy and beauty of the single life, but then she called me several months later to say she had just gotten engaged. And try telling single parents that God is calling or sending them forth to raise their kids on their own. "Thanks a lot, God!" might be their sarcastic reply.

On top of the feedback everyone else was giving me on the question of vocation and mission, my own experience was telling me that God was not sitting somewhere holding a list with my name on it (or not on it, for that matter) with the vocation/mission I was supposed to be following. For one thing, I obviously had many different kinds of work going on in my life. Some of my jobs were interesting and fulfilling and socially meaningful, and others were not. I was married, divorced, and had no children. Then I became happily married and had three children in twenty months. Was I called to the married and parental state all along, or only when I was successful at it?

Finally, I came to the conclusion that the concept of mission or vocation was not a useful one in my life. If everything that anyone does is a vocation, then it is a pretty meaningless concept. If, on the other hand, only certain people have a vocation and most don't, then it is an elitist and ultimately not very helpful concept.

. . .

Recently, however, I have been working with young adults—my own three children and many others. It strikes me that one of the things young people are looking for is a vocation or mission worthy of their lives. They may not articulate this, but as they are deciding whether or not to go to college, what to study or major in, what kind of job or career they might pursue, whether or not they want to get married, what kind of person they might want to marry, whether or not they might want to have children and how they would want to raise their children, where they might want to live, how to take care of their aging parents (actually, they don't think about that last one at all), they are really asking what their vocation or mission in life might be.

This led me to revisit my own understanding of the vocation/mission question, and I finally asked it the right way. What I asked myself was this: is there anything in my life that I have always felt called or compelled to do, any drive or impulse that I have ultimately been unable to ignore? The answer was that yes, there is. Ever since I was a young man, I have felt the strongest of urges to try to help make the world a better place. I don't know exactly where this feeling comes from. I am sure it is in great part due to my parents and the rest of my family and friends, to my wife and children, to my education and the countless books I have read, and to what I have learned sitting through literally thousands of Masses and religious education classes and programs.

I have no other imperative in my life that is as strong as this one, except maybe survival and protecting my children. It is so strong, in fact, that—for the first time in my life—I feel comfortable in calling it a vocation or mission from God. I can ignore it, but it does not go away. I am happier when I am following it than when I am not. It is something that gives integrity and meaning to all the other choices I make in my life.

Could it be that I have had this vocation/mission all my life and have just never been able to recognize or articulate it? Could it be that all people have such a calling, such a mission worthy of their life, embedded in their very soul?

. . .

Certainly, people would differ in how they describe their vocation/mission. Some might say they are driven to creating beauty, and everything in their lives revolves around that. Others might cite fighting for freedom or justice, or pursuing adventure, or sating their intellectual curiosity. Some might name developing relations among family or friends as their guiding principle, while still others might describe their vocation/mission as serving others.

Are all of these the same vocation? I am tempted to say that they are, but I don't want to presume. The key element, however, would be that the vocation/mission initiated with God and culminates with God as well. It is the strength, the inevitability, and the persistence of the call or commission that determine its divine origin.

What about vocations/missions that are not from God? What if someone really feels, for example, that his or her purpose in life is to make as much money as possible, and that nothing else much matters? But since a vocation/mission is

between ourselves and God, perhaps there is no way of ultimately deceiving ourselves on this issue. In other words, the
only true vocation/mission is the one God gives us, and God
gives each one of us a vocation/mission that is truly worthy of our lives. We either accept it or we don't, discern it or
not. But it is not something we can make up or kid ourselves
about.

Does everyone have a vocation/mission? I now say yes,
almost unequivocally. Do we all recognize, understand, and
accept that vocation/mission? No, at least not on a conscious
level. But we may act on it in any case. Is everyone's vocation/
mission the same? Not in the sense that we would explain or
describe it in the same words, but certainly in the sense that
St. Paul described: "We know that God is always at work for
the good of everyone who loves him. They are the ones God
has chosen for his purpose, and he has always known who his
chosen ones would be" (Rom 8:28-29). For how could God's
callings or commissions be at cross-purposes to one another?

This sense of vocation/mission is critical when it comes
to practicing the spirituality of work, for unless we are clear
about it, we cannot see how our daily work—both of the
paid and the unpaid variety—serves our greater purpose in
life. And when it comes time for the Dismissal from Mass,
we have to know what we are being sent forth to do: we are
not merely being dismissed to go do our various jobs; we are
being sent forth to fulfill our shared vocation/mission to help
make the world more like God—the Father, the Almighty, the
maker of heaven and earth—would have it. That is truly a
mission worthy of anyone's life.

A Story about Vocation/Mission

Four stone masons were working on a cathedral. "I am making a good living," said the first. "I am building a cathedral," said the second. "I am pursuing my career," said the third. "I feel compelled to make beautiful things," said the fourth. All four were called by God. All four were sent by God. All four fulfilled God's purpose: The cathedral was built, it was beautiful, and the world was a better place because of it.

Questions for Reflection and Discussion

1. Is there anything you feel compelled to do, whether you have to or not, whether anyone sees it or not? What is it? Where do you think that drive comes from? Why?

2. How do the various jobs and volunteer activities you do fit in with the overall sense of purpose in your life? What do you do when you find they don't?

3. Give an example of a true vocation/mission from God and an example of a false one. Use examples from your own life if you have them. How can you tell the difference between a true and a false vocation/mission? How do you know one is from God and the other is not?

two

....

The Kingdom of God

....

THE WAY SAINT Luke tells it in the beginning verses of the Acts of the Apostles, Jesus gets one more shot at training his disciples during the forty days between the resurrection and the ascension. Of course, that means he gets one more shot at training us, his modern disciples.

What will he tell us? Of all the things we need to know, what will be the most important? Will it be about how to pray? Or what the next life will be like? Or how we might save our immortal souls?

These might have been good things for Jesus to talk about, but Luke does not record that he did. Instead, he says very simply that Jesus spent those forty days talking with the disciples about the most important thing to him, the center of the mission on which he was sending us, the entire reason he had been sent into the world, died for us, and been raised from the dead. "He appeared to his apostles," Luke writes, "and spoke to them about God's kingdom" (Acts 1:3).

There it is, as simple and as profound as Jesus himself. He spoke to us about the same thing he had always talked about. It was the mission that the Father had sent him to begin, and he was now sending the disciples to continue that same mission. They (we) were to make disciples of all nations so that the mission could go on into the unnamed future, until it is gloriously brought to completion and Christ can return in full glory.

. . .

What is that mission we humans are supposed to help accomplish? We are to help bring about the kingdom of God "on earth as it is in heaven," as Jesus taught us to pray. No more, and no less.

How are we supposed to carry out that mission? This is a much more difficult question. It is no wonder the disciples locked themselves back up in the upper room after Jesus left. But then there occurred that great pentecost event, when the Holy Spirit blew down the doors and filled the disciples (i.e., us) with the courage and knowledge and wisdom to go forth and proclaim this new way of doing business.

But again, how are we supposed to help bring about the kingdom of God on earth as it is in heaven? Many people assume that the kingdom of God occurs only in the next life, but Jesus was pretty clear that the reign of God was to be realized on this earth and among the human race. Otherwise, the Our Father would say, "Thy kingdom come, thy will be done, in heaven as it is in heaven," which makes no sense. Besides, if you look at Jesus' descriptions of the kingdom of God, they are all about how we are to act in this life: The kingdom of God is like a mustard seed, like a man who had two sons, like a woman who had ten coins; the kingdom of God has already begun, it is coming when we least expect it, it is within us, it is not for us to know the time and place when it will be realized.

More than anything else, the kingdom of God is about us "bearing fruit." What is important is that we take the talents we have been given and do something with them. It is the doing something with our talents that constitutes our work, and it is our work that will help make the world more like the way God would have things.

. . .

The phrase "the kingdom of God" (or "the kingdom of heaven," where God is in charge) appears about one hundred fifty times in the New Testament, in virtually every book and letter. There is only one logical explanation for this: It is there because Jesus himself used the words to describe what he and his mission were all about.

What does it mean, this "kingdom of God"? Some Christians over the centuries have taken it to mean that there should be a virtual theocracy, that God should "reign" like a king—albeit using religious and political leaders as surrogates. This concept has led to all kinds of weird ideas, including the Crusades, the Holy Roman Empire, the Papal States, etc. Even today, some people in democracies like the United States feel that the kingdom of God would occur if only they or the people they support could get into office and run things the way they want them run. In fact, the kingdom of God can be a very dangerous image. It has led to a lot of triumphalism throughout history, and it can be used as a way of saying, "My religion is better than your religion," or "My God is better than your God."

It is very doubtful that this is what Jesus had in mind. His idea of the kingdom of God was one in which the "blessed" were the poor, the meek, the people who mourn, those who suffer persecution, those who hunger and thirst for justice. He seemed to show virtually no interest in politics or civic affairs. What he was interested in was the conversion and subsequent transformation of people who were formerly blind but now could see. He was interested in the turning of our hearts and minds toward God. Once this was accomplished, he apparently thought, everything else would follow.

When the disciples asked Jesus to teach them how to pray, which curiously is recorded as having occurred only once, it is interesting to analyze exactly what he said (see Matthew 6:9-13). First he said that we should pray to "our Father," that is, that same God "in heaven" that Jesus knew, the one whose very name is "hallowed" or "holy." Then, the very next words out of our mouths, according to Jesus, should be to ask that God's kingdom come (that is, that God's will be done) "on earth as it is in heaven." In fact, all we need besides God's kingdom is our basic necessities (our daily bread); to be forgiven (to the same extent that we forgive others); to be kept free of temptation (perhaps the temptation to build our own kingdom rather than that of God); and to be delivered from all evil (which is what happens when God's kingdom is not yet a reality).

Although Jesus told Pilate, "My kingdom does not belong to this world" (Jn 18:36), the only logical conclusion is that Jesus did not have a political kingdom in mind, but very much expected the kingdom to be "in" this world, if not "of" it.

• • •

So if Jesus' kingdom of God is to come in this world, if it is not a political or temporal kingdom, if it is aimed especially at those who are oppressed by the way things are, and if we have been sent on the mission by Jesus to help bring it about, how are we to do it?

We do it through our work—our work as parents and children and family and friends, our work as citizens and members of our civic communities; our work as members of our local, diocesan, and universal churches; and especially our work on our jobs, both paid and unpaid.

That is why there has to be a spirituality of work, and that is why we have to learn to practice it. If work is truly the centerpiece of a life's mission, then we have got to figure out ways of doing it in such a way that it does, in fact, help bring about the kingdom of God . . . in this world, not in the next.

A Story about the Kingdom of God and Work

Eons ago, God decided to create a universe. Whether God has ever done this before or since, we'll never know. What we do know, however, is that God created beings to help finish the job.

The first couple of beings off the assembly line were slightly flawed. They didn't seem to like the idea of doing what they were told, and so they didn't.

Initially, God was angry about this flaw and wanted to start over. But then God said, "Maybe it would be interesting to create a universe using flawed workers."

So the beings began working to complete the creation they had been given. And God looked at it and saw that it was good, but flawed as you might expect. So God became one of the beings in order to tell them exactly the kind of universe God had in mind. Some of them believed and began building the universe to God's specifications, others have not yet believed and continue to build the universe to their own specifications.

How this is all going to end is still in doubt, but there is some indication that those beings who follow God's way of doing things will win out in the end. Other evidence, however, points to the opposite conclusion. The final arbiters, apparently, will be the flawed beings themselves.

Questions for Reflection and Discussion
....

1. What do you think is the purpose or meaning of life? What is the purpose or meaning of your specific life?

2. What other images or words could you use to describe what Jesus had in mind with the phrase "kingdom of God"? How could that reality ever come about in the world?

3. Rewrite the Our Father in your own words. Do not use any of the specific phrasing you already know, but instead put the prayer in different words that still make sense to you.

three

Mission Impossible

THERE IS ONE huge problem with making the kingdom of God the mission that defines our entire lives: This idea of trying to make the earth into a place where God's will is done all the time (as it is in heaven) is simply not going to work. You know it; I know it; history knows it. It is an impossible mission.

First of all, if it were going to happen, it should have happened by now. The Christian enterprise has been at it for over two thousand years, and it could be argued that things are as bad as they ever were. Certainly, no one would argue that we are right on the edge of success in bringing about the kingdom. Just list all the bad things in this world right now: war, terrorism, poverty, hunger, racism, abortion, capital punishment, injustice of so many kinds. If we are supposed to be fixing all these things, we have been huge failures.

Second, most of us are not in a position to do much about anything that is wrong with the world anyway. We don't have much power in our personal lives, and even in our public lives it often seems that what we say or do doesn't really matter very much.

Third, we are not the only ones around. We exist in a world that has become much smaller and yet more pluralistic. We are confronted every day with the knowledge that there are a lot of people in the world who do not believe or think the way we do and, in fact, view many things very differently than we do. How are we Christians supposed to bring about the kingdom of God on earth when we can't even agree—even among ourselves—what the kingdom of God might look like? And should we impose our vision on others, even if we could?

So why even try? If we know we have failed and most likely will fail, why even try to carry out a mission thought up by some young Jewish idealist over two thousand years ago? Why fight impossible odds against forces that are much stronger than we are? Why continue to push a rock up a hill, knowing that it is going to roll back down to the bottom every time?

These are good questions. Fortunately, the Mass provides some very good answers.

· · ·

The Mass tells us that the bringing about of the kingdom is God's job, not ours. "For the kingdom, and the power, and the glory are yours, now and for ever," we pray at the end of the Our Father. Jesus never intended that any one person or any single group of us would be able to pull off this mission. He was pretty clear that the kingdom would come in its own time, a time that even he did not know. And he knew that the coming of the kingdom was not a human endeavor. That is why we needed the Holy Spirit. In fact, Jesus said that the reason he had to leave was so that the Holy Spirit would come. It was almost as if Jesus understood that even he could not bring about the kingdom and that he had to get off the scene so that the Spirit could do it.

That is not to say that God does not need us. Perhaps "need" is too strong a word, because it is hard to imagine that God needs human beings. But if we are to believe Jesus (and as Peter said, where else are we to turn?), somehow it is God's plan to use "the work of human hands" to bring about this celestial kingdom on earth. The Mass makes this point over and over: our work is acceptable, our failures are forgiven, we are sent forth. We may think our efforts are worthless, but God does not. Catholics believe that when we eat the body and blood of Christ we become Christ to the world. It is Christ-in-us or us-as-Christ that is being sent forth to transform the world. Maybe he can succeed through us.

. . .

The other thing that the Mass teaches us is that we are not sent on this mission as individuals. One of the hallmarks of Catholicism is its universality. Catholicism is for everyone and is found everywhere (that's what "catholic" means), and no matter where you find Catholics you will find the Mass, and at the end of the Mass everyone present will be sent forth to carry out the mission that Jesus sent us all on.

What this means is that it almost doesn't matter what any one of us (or any single parish or diocese or even country) does. The job of transforming the world is shared with everyone else who is being sent forth, both vertically (throughout history) and horizontally (across the globe). What we each do and how we do it is important, of course, but it is all part of God's plan, which none of us comprehend. As God says in the Book of Isaiah, "My thoughts and my ways are not like yours. Just as the heavens are higher than the earth, my thoughts and my ways are higher than yours" (Is 55:8-9).

Maybe this is a way of looking at the classic "faith vs. works" dispute between Catholics and some of our Protestant brethren. While this is often set in personal terms about individual salvation, perhaps it could also be seen in corporate terms regarding our mission to the world. While we are all expected to participate in the mission (and do our "good works"), it is "by faith alone" that we believe that the kingdom of God will ever come. In other words, our individual good works are not going to transform the world, but we believe that somehow God will use our collective efforts to accomplish that mission.

· · ·

The Mass is designed to prevent us from being discouraged on the one hand and self-righteous on the other. We are not going to accomplish God's mission through our own efforts, but all our efforts are being used by the Spirit to accomplish that mission in God's own good time.

The Mass is kind of like the day that Bill Murray has in the movie *Groundhog Day*. Every day his alarm clock goes off and he goes through the exact same set of experiences. Eventually, he learns that his actions do matter and that he can change both himself and those around him for the better. The Mass is similar. For two thousand years we have been sending people forth "to love and serve the Lord." Sometimes we do it right, sometimes we blow it completely; most of the time we do a middling job. But the Mass goes on, day after day, week after week, millennium after millennium, and somehow out of all that sending forth, God's kingdom has already begun, even though it has not yet come.

St. Vincent de Paul had a saying: "Let us do the good that presents itself." That is a good description of what we are being sent forth from Mass to do. If we all go forth "to love and serve the Lord," we will all try to do the good that presents itself. Some days we will succeed; others, we will fail. In the process, God's kingdom will come, on earth as it is in heaven.

A Story about Mission Impossible

"Your mission, should you choose to accept it, is to make the world more like the way God wants it to be."

"But how am I to accomplish that mission?"

"That information is classified, but there are others who have been sent on the mission with you. Some you will know; others you will not. Eventually, we all will succeed."

"Will I see the victory?"

"You already have."

Questions for Reflection and Discussion

1. Describe times when you have felt that it was impossible for you to act as a Christian in your daily life. Describe other times when you have done so. What caused the difference?

2. Have you ever experienced the kingdom of God in your home, neighborhood, or workplace? What was it like? How long did it last? What happened to it?

3. Does the Mass help you deal with how you carry out your mission to the world? Why or why not? Describe what you would need to sustain your sense of mission throughout the week.

part two

....

The Mass as a
Sending Forth

....

....

four

The Sending Forth

....

NEAR THE END of Mass, my three young adult children lean over and ask for the car keys. They want to get out and get going as soon as possible. My wife and I tell them, "No, the most important part of the Mass is coming. We cannot leave until we have been sent forth." They look at us with the look only young people can muster that silently says, "Whatever," and wait the extra minute or two until the Mass is over and they can take off.

In some ways, however, the kids have the right idea. The point of the Mass is not to hang around church afterwards, but to go back to our daily lives renewed and recommitted to our mission as followers of Jesus. But in other ways, our children have missed the point of the entire Mass if they leave before the Dismissal.

Their mistake is understandable. First, they see many of their elders heading for the exits, some as early as right after communion. Second, they have never been taught why the

Dismissal is such an important part of the Mass. And finally, in our parish (and in most churches they have attended), the Dismissal is done in such a perfunctory manner that it is hard for anyone to take it seriously. (In fact, it is often immediately preceded by a mind-numbingly long list of parish announcements.)

But if our three young adults ever get the real idea behind the Dismissal, then they will realize why it is such a vital part of the Mass and so critical to how they live their lives and do their work. The Dismissal will become such an integral part of their practice of the spirituality of work that they will want to stay and participate in the final sending forth, which is what the entire Mass really is meant to be.

• • •

The word *Mass* actually comes from the Latin words for the Dismissal, *"Ite, missa est,"* which mean "Go, we are sent forth." Sometime in church history, some people thought this was an important enough part of the liturgy to name the entire thing after it. (Hence, the word *Mass* is from the Latin *missa*.) The Latin verb on which *missa* is based is *mitto, mittere,* which was originally a military term that had the connotation "to throw or to hurl." Thus we get the modern English word *missile* from the same verb. We also get the words *mission, missionary,* and *dismissal.* So the Dismissal from Mass originally meant that we were being "shot like out of a cannon" back into the world to carry out a "mission" that was central to why we had come together to celebrate the Mass in the first place.

What is that mission? It is as amazing as it is obvious and misunderstood. It is the very mission on which Jesus sent his disciples over two thousand years ago. That mission, as we have seen, is no less than to transform the world into a place much more like the way God would have things.

This mission is, of course, impossible on the face of it. Not only is it obvious that we, the "people of God," have not succeeded the entire time we have been on this mission, but it is also obvious that we will not succeed in accomplishing it in the future. So why even try?

We try because Jesus asked us to try. In the Acts of the Apostles, Luke says, "For forty days after Jesus had suffered and died, he proved in many ways that he had been raised from death. He appeared to his apostles and spoke to them about God's kingdom" (Acts 1:3). Imagine that! Of all the things that Jesus could have spoken to his disciples about, he picked one thing and one thing only: the reign of God.

. . .

So when we are sent forth from the Mass, we are sent forth to go out and try again to help transform the world along the lines that God intended and Jesus preached. When looked at the right way, as "The Sending Forth," the Mass is the perfect liturgy to help us accomplish this "mission impossible."

And here is the best part. It doesn't matter whether or not the priest or deacon or liturgist or homilist or presider or leader of song is clear on this. Of course, if they are, it would make things easier for us. But all we laypeople have to do is be aware that the Mass is designed to send us forth (back into the world), and it will do its job. That's how cool the Mass is.

A Story about the Sending Forth

"This Sunday," said the presider, "we are going to honor all those in the congregation whose primary ministry is out in the world, helping to make the world more like the way things are in heaven, where God's will is always done. Will everyone in the congregation who participates in that ministry please come up around the altar so that the rest of us can bless you?"

When all those who participated in the ministry of the sending forth had come up around the altar, there was no one left in the pews to bless them.

Questions for Reflection and Discussion

1. What are you being sent forth from Mass to do, and where are you being sent forth to do it? Be specific, and do not use the words "to love and serve the Lord."

2. In what ways does your work on your job, with your family, and in your community help build the kingdom of God on earth? In what ways does it prevent the kingdom from coming to fruition?

3. On a scale of 1-10, with 10 being the full realization of the kingdom of God, where are the following: your home; your workplace; your neighborhood; your city, state, country; the world? In each case, why, and what might you do to raise the score?

five

The Coming Back

IN TODAY'S LITURGY, the Dismissal comes near the end of the Mass, immediately after the priest's final blessing. The priest (or deacon) says, "Go in the peace of Christ," or "The Mass is ended, go in peace," or "Go in peace to love and serve the Lord," and we all reply, "Thanks be to God." There is nothing wrong with these words in and of themselves, although they lack some of the urgency of the Latin, *"Ite, missa est,"* which can almost be translated: "Go, what are you standing around for? Get out of here. You are being sent forth to do something. Go do it!"

It is unfortunate that the Dismissal is done so poorly in most parishes. First, it is often preceded or immediately followed by a long list of announcements about parish programs and activities. Nothing is wrong with this in and of itself, but it does tend to trivialize and lessen the impact of the Dismissal. Second, the priest (or deacon) who delivers the words of Dismissal often does so in a voice without excitement or conviction, and the response of the congregation is almost equally uninspired—sounding almost like we are thanking God that the Mass is over, rather than for the mission worthy of our lives on which we have just been sent.

The English words for Dismissal are also unfortunate. "Go in peace to love and serve the Lord," is a fine sentiment, but unless it is carefully unpacked, it can sound as bland as, "Let us go and be nice people," or even "Goodbye; have a nice day." And the response of "Thanks be to God," besides being used often throughout the Mass, is perhaps not the best reaction to being asked to perform an impossible task. "Lord, have mercy!" or even, "No, thanks, I tried that, and it didn't work," might be a more honest response.

But the real problem with the Dismissal is that it is viewed as an isolated act that comes at the end of a fairly long liturgy and seems disconnected from what went before. The Dismissal should be the culmination of all that has happened before it, and my kids and fellow parishioners shouldn't dream of leaving before it occurs. Perhaps the Dismissal shouldn't even be at the end of the Mass, although that is probably too much to ask of our liturgists, but at the very least the Dismissal should be on everyone's mind throughout the liturgy, so that when it occurs, its significance cannot be missed. Here is a look at the Mass through the lens of the Dismissal, as if it were the most important part of the Mass.

· · ·

Looking through the lens of the Dismissal, Catholics would never *go* to Mass or *come* to Mass or *attend* Mass. Except for the very first time, which for most of us was in childhood, we Catholics would *come back* to Mass. We are coming back from having been *sent forth* from the previous Mass we attended.

There is no one who is exempt from this mission, from the priest and parish staff to every single member of the congregation. The mission is not to the parish or church or even to parish-sponsored ministries. The mission is to the world, including our jobs, our families and friends, our community and civic involvements. It is by virtue of our baptism and confirmation that we have been chosen for and accepted this mission. It is not optional, nor is it reserved for religious professionals or even the especially pious or holy. We were *all* sent forth, and now we are *all* returning from the mission.

So like the good friends and colleagues in mission that we are, we greet one another and sing a song. (Some parishes even have greeters at the doors to welcome people to Mass. If they had the Dismissal in mind, the greeters would be saying "Welcome back" rather than "Hello" or "Good Morning.") Because our mission is important and because we know that the Mass is directly related to helping us carry it out, most of us would be on time most of the time. Having been in the "mission fields" for a while, we would know the importance of a liturgy that was designed to celebrate our (few) victories and lick the wounds of our (many) failures. We would also know that we were going to be sent forth in an hour or so to carry out exactly the same mission we have been on all week, so we need all the help we can get before we go.

• • •

We finish the opening hymn, the presider welcomes us and reads a short prayer, and then we get our first reminder that we are going to be sent forth again. The priest suggests that we have all failed in some way, and we all agree. There is no show of hands for those who have sinned and those who have not. We each admit that we have failed in many ways, "in what I have done, and in what I have failed to do." Through the lens of the Dismissal, the main thing we have "failed to do" is to bring about that kingdom of God we were sent forth to help inaugurate. Oh, we may have tried. We may even have

succeeded in some (usually small) ways. But overall and cor-
porately, we have failed on the mission on which we were
sent just a few days earlier.

Surprisingly, however, we don't beat ourselves up about it.
Instead, we ask for forgiveness—from God, from one another,
from ourselves. We ask our Blessed Mother, the angels and
saints, and our "brothers and sisters" present with us to "pray
for me to the Lord, our God." The priest asks God to "have
mercy on us, forgive us our sins, and bring us to everlasting
life." We all recall that we are a forgiven people and are not
expected to succeed all the time. We pray or sing, "Lord, have
mercy." And then, surprisingly, we are forgiven. It is as easy
as that, partly because—from the point of view of the Dismissal—we know we are going to be sent forth again soon
and will have another chance.

Suddenly, we are so happy that we start singing again.
This time it is the "Glory to God," the ancient hymn of all
Christians to express our joy at being part of the entire enterprise. We are in a line of over two thousand years of people
coming together and then being sent forth again. So we give
thanks to our God "in the highest" and ask for "peace to his
people on earth." Remember: In a little while we will be sent
forth in that same peace "to love and serve" that same Lord.
From the point of view of the Dismissal, our time together is
already running out, and we still have a lot of work to do.

A Story about Coming Back

The young college student finally went to Mass at her
school. Her parents had been bugging her to go, but that was
not the reason she went.

She went because she felt defeated, empty, unhappy. College was not what she had hoped it would be. She couldn't remember why she had chosen this place. She didn't know what she wanted to study or why. It was all too overwhelming for her.

When she walked into the church, however, she felt as if she had come home. She saw a lot of people who were just like her, and some of them looked lost too.

The presider started the Mass with a flourish. "We are going to send ourselves back out into the world in about an hour," he said, "to transform it into a place much more like God would have it. We have all failed in this mission since the last time we were together, but God forgives us and we must forgive ourselves."

"Lord, have mercy," the girl said to herself.

Questions for Reflection or Discussion

1. How well have you carried out your mission to help transform the world? Have you forgiven yourself for your failures, for "what you have done" and "what you have failed to do"? Name some of those things.

2. What would happen if every single person in your church felt that he or she was returning from having been sent on a mission from God? Describe how that would change the nature of your worship services.

3. If people actually tried to bring about the kingdom of God on their jobs, with their families, and in their communities each week, how would they feel by the time they returned to Mass? Would they be willing to be sent forth again right away? What would they need first?

six

Preparing to Be Sent Forth Again

AS THE MASS continues, we've just admitted we have failed on our mission, reminded ourselves that we are forgiven for our failures, and given glory to God. But we are about to be sent forth again on the same mission, and we know what is in store for us. At most Catholic churches, we've only got about 45-50 minutes left before the Dismissal. If we are going to do a better job next time, we need to better prepare ourselves, and what better way than to look in the Good Book itself—the Bible, the divinely inspired work of God?

And so we move the focus over to the other side of the altar and have two or three readings, one or two from the Old Testament or the non-gospel books of the New Testament, and always one reading from the gospels. The church provides us with a three-year cycle that ensures we read most of the gospels at least every three years and tries to connect the other readings to the gospels whenever possible.

From the point of view of the Dismissal, however, the important thing is what we are looking for in the readings. What we are looking for is *advice* and *inspiration* for carrying out the mission we are about to be sent forth upon.

Sometimes this advice is easy to understand; other times it takes a little more work to apply it to our immediate situation. Sometimes one reading will speak to us; other times another will. When we're really paying attention, sometimes all three readings will strike us as being directly about how we are to live our lives in the carrying out of our mission. So we say "Thanks be to God" at the end of the first two readings (the same as we will say when we are sent forth at the Dismissal), and "Praise to you, Lord Jesus Christ" at the end of the gospel reading, because it truly is Jesus' mission we are going on, and he is telling and showing us exactly how to do it.

Now, if we could only have some help in understanding the readings. . . .

• • •

When seen through the lens of the Dismissal, the purpose of the homily is very clear. We are all about to be sent forth on a mission. We have just heard two or three readings that were the divinely inspired "word of God." Unfortunately, these writings were made two thousand to four thousand years ago, in specific historical circumstances, by writers with their own culturally determined concerns, assumptions, references, and biases. If the readings were easy to understand, we wouldn't need a homily at all. But most laypeople know that we need someone to "break open" the word of God, as they say in preaching school. We need someone who has the knowledge, the skill, and the time to reflect on the scriptures ahead of time and then help us make the connection between what the Bible has to say and . . . and what?

If you are looking at the Mass with the Dismissal in mind, the answer is that we need the homilist to make the connection between the readings and the mission on which we are going to be sent once again . . . in about half an hour or so.

There are some obvious problems with this understanding of the homily. First, let's be honest that some of the more esoteric readings from the scriptures are tough to relate to the contemporary world, or they deal with issues that no longer seem important, or they are just plain hard to understand (e.g., much of the Book of Revelation, Deuteronomy, Numbers, etc.). The church in its wisdom always provides two or three readings, including one from the gospels, so usually a good homilist can work around this problem.

A much more serious concern, however, is whether or not the homilist is able to relate the readings to the Dismissal. Some homilists are so isolated from the real world of work, family, and civic affairs that they are not even sure what issues people are facing in their daily lives as they try to apply the scripture readings to their mission in the world. In this case it is right and good that the homilist seek the help of ordinary laypeople in preparing the homily, either by talking with them, visiting them in their workplaces, or at least reading books by and about the laity.

Even more problematic, from the Dismissal viewpoint, are those preachers who aren't clear that they are about to send the congregation forth on a mission and that the homily is an integral part of that responsibility. If a preacher does not have the Dismissal in mind during the preparation and delivery of a homily, then there is no way that the connection with the mission will be made. In fact, each homily should mention something like: "We are about to be sent forth to carry out the mission Jesus asked us to undertake, so we had best pay attention to these readings."

. . .

Right after the homily on most Sundays, we say the Nicene Creed together. This, too, can seem a little hard to understand, because it deals with a lot of the issues of faith that faced the early church. For example, the fact that Jesus was "begotten, not made" was very important in the third century, but it is maybe not as much a concern to the average Christian in the twenty-first century (partly, perhaps, because it was resolved back then).

Through the lens of the Dismissal, however, saying the creed is merely making sure we are all on the same page before we head out on our mission. The specifics may not be as important as the fact that we are saying it together. To be honest, some of us just let the words of the creed wash over us like a familiar blanket. It's not so much that we are assenting to every statement as we are assenting to being part of a two-thousand-year-old church that is still sending us on the same mission Jesus gave to his original disciples. With the creed we agree: We believe in the one, true God; we believe in his Son, Jesus, through whom "all things were made" and whose "kingdom will have no end"; we believe in the Holy Spirit, the "giver of life" who "has spoken through the Prophets"; we believe in the "one, holy, catholic, and apostolic" church that is about to send us forth; and we acknowledge our "one baptism" by virtue of which we are called to carry out our mission to help bring about "the life of the world to come."

So the creed is important in terms of the Dismissal in that it identifies our basic beliefs and who we are as a people as we are about to be commissioned once again to go forth "to love and serve the Lord."

. . .

If we want to turn the Mass into a sending forth, the Prayer of the Faithful or General Intercessions offer a perfect opportunity, because they are one of the few parts of the Mass that are not pretty rigidly specified. This is, after all, our prayer, the prayer of the laity in the pew. Supposedly, we can pray for whatever it is we need. If we are about to go on an important mission (which we are), then much of the prayer of the faithful should be aimed at helping us carry out that mission.

Here are some sample prayers of the faithful with the Dismissal firmly in mind. (Response is "Equip Us, Lord.")

> That we might help bring about your kingdom on our jobs by how we perform our work and the example we give to others, we pray to the Lord.
>
> That we might help bring about your kingdom in our homes and with our families by how we treat one another, and the generosity we show to our neighbors and those less fortunate than we are, we pray to the Lord.
>
> That we might help bring about your kingdom in our neighborhoods, city, state, and nation by being involved in civic affairs and performing our duties as citizens, we pray to the Lord.
>
> That we might be sent forth from this Mass as if we had been shot from a cannon to carry out our mission in and to the world, we pray to the Lord.

· · ·

You get the idea. There are thousands of prayers we can make that will remind the faithful that we are being sent forth to do something important. Sometimes we might pray for those in a particular profession or occupation, such as lawyers or nurses or city workers. Other times we might ask for help with specific problems, such as famine or corporate corruption or war. But all our prayers of the faithful need to be put in the context of the Dismissal.

Should we also pray for the pope, the bishop, the pastor, other church ministers? Of course we should. They are key to sending us on our mission. Should we also pray for the sick and those who have died? No doubt. They are no longer available for mission duty and will be missed. The primary purpose of each prayer of the faithful from the point of view of the Dismissal, however, is for help on the mission on which we are being sent.

A Story about the Word

In the beginning is the Word. And the Word is with God. And the Word is God.

Through the Word all things are made new, and without the Word not one thing is made new.

What is made new through the Word is life, and that life is the light of the world. And the light comes into the darkness, but the darkness neither comprehends the light nor overcomes it.

And the Word becomes flesh and blood through the work of human hands and minds and hearts and spirits, and that Word dwells among us.

Questions for Reflection or Discussion

....

1. When was the last time you heard a homily that was connected with the Dismissal? What was such a homily like, or what could one be like?

2. How do the scriptures help prepare you for your mission to help make the world a better place? How could they be more helpful to you? What can you do to make sure that happens?

3. Write your own Prayer of the Faithful, with your own daily work in mind.

seven

....

Transubstantiating Our Gifts

....

THE MASS CONTINUES. We are now done with the Liturgy of the Word and are at the main altar. The Dismissal is coming up fast, but we still have several tasks to do before we leave. And so we participate in the Liturgy of the Eucharist, which means the liturgy of thanks. We are thankful for many things, of course, but through the lens of the Dismissal we are especially thankful for the worthy mission on which we are about to be sent.

And so we offer the gifts we have brought. It is not our money (although that is certainly part of our offering), nor is it animal sacrifice. Following the lead of Jesus, we offer bread ("which earth has given and human hands have made") and wine ("fruit of the vine and work of human hands"). In other words, we offer processed food—not ingredients, just found in nature. We offer bread and wine, not wheat and grapes. Nor is it just the work of the baker and vintner that we offer.

We offer all the work of human hands and minds and hearts and bodies.

In fact, what we offer is the imperfect work that we have all done since the last time we were sent forth. We have already admitted that work was flawed and been forgiven for it, but now we have the temerity to offer it to God. "Pray, my brothers and sisters, that our sacrifice may be acceptable," the priest asks, and we respond, "May the Lord accept the sacrifice at your hands . . . for our good, and the good of all his church."

And guess what? The gift is found acceptable. Instead of being the punishment for our sins, which have now been forgiven anyway, our daily work has become our offering to God, been accepted, and is about to be turned into much, much more. And so we pray or sing the "Holy, holy, holy," where we acknowledge that "heaven *and* earth are full of God's glory."

· · ·

The priest then takes our gifts, prays over them, and says the words of consecration, transforming (or transubstantiating, if you are a student of Thomas Aquinas) our gifts (our daily work) into the body and blood of Jesus, into divine life itself. We proclaim this mystery of faith: "Lord, by your cross and resurrection, you have set us free. You are the Savior of the world." And the priest prays to God, "Through Christ our Lord you give us all these gifts. You fill them with life and goodness, you bless them and make them holy."

So our work has been accepted, made holy, and transformed into the holy of holies. What else can we do but say or sing the great "Amen" or "So be it," for we are once again going to be sent out on our mission and are accepting it wholeheartedly (if with some trepidation). There are only a few minutes left before we are dismissed, and there are only a couple of tasks left to accomplish.

. . .

First, we need to remind ourselves what that mission is. It is easy to get confused, what with all the mixed signals we receive from both the church and the world. So we go back to the source, to the prayer that Jesus gave us, and we pray, "Our Father." Not "my father," or "your father," or "somebody else's father." We pray to the Father of us all, the one who is "in heaven" (where the true God dwells), and we bless his name. And then we pray, "thy kingdom come—thy will be done (it's the same thing)—on earth as it is in heaven." There it is: a mission truly worthy of our lives, and we are all going to be sent forth to accomplish it.

Next, we ask for our daily bread, which is the work that each of us is given to do, the work "of human hands" that we will bring back to the next Mass and offer as our gift. We ask once again for forgiveness, because we know that we will fail in our mission, and we promise to be as forgiving of others as we want to be forgiven ourselves. Finally, we ask that we not be led into the temptation that we know the world offers, and that the Father will deliver us from the many evils we know are out there in the world.

For it is not *our* kingdom that we are trying to build, for "The kingdom, and the power and the glory are *yours*, now and forever."

A Story about Transubstantiation

The little drummer boy came to the stable and said, "I have no gifts to lay before the king."

Mary smiled and said, "You must play your drum for the baby." And so the little drummer boy's beat was transformed into gold, frankincense, and myrrh.

Questions for Reflection and Discussion

1. What is your "work of human hands" that you offer to God at Mass? Describe how you feel about what you are offering. Is your work good enough to offer to God? Why or why not? How does it feel to know that your work is found acceptable and will be transformed into the body and blood of Christ?

2. Say the Our Father, but skip the words, "thy will be done." How does the prayer strike you now? Do you believe that God's will could ever be done "on earth as it is in heaven"? Describe what that might look like.

3. Read the alternative Eucharistic Prayer by Edward Schillebeeckx in appendix #2. Would you want it used at Mass? Why or why not?

eight

....

Food for the Journey

....

THE MASS IS almost at the end, and we are just about ready to be dismissed. Through the lens of the Dismissal, we are going to be sent forth, shot out of a cannon to go and do an impossible task. So we turn to our fellow missionaries and say goodbye and good luck. This is the kiss of peace.

We do this with some strange words, however. We remember that Jesus said to his disciples, "I leave you peace, my peace I give you." We ask that Jesus "grant us the peace and unity of your kingdom, where you live for ever and ever." It is the peace of the Lord that we give each other, a peace that is not like the peace the world gives, but a special kind of peace—perhaps a peace that allows us to carry out our mission against impossible odds.

"Peace be with you," we say (that word *peace* is going to come up again in the Dismissal). "And also with you," we respond. No one is exempt from this farewell. We are all being sent forth on the same mission.

But before we go on our journey, we need some food, and it must be special food indeed, for it needs to sustain us until the next time we get together for Mass.

• • •

The eucharistic bread is broken and the consecrated wine poured in preparation for Communion. We are all getting ready to eat, because we are all going on a journey. We are reminded that this bread and wine is "the Lamb of God," who *always* and *already* "takes away the sins of the world." Those of us who have been called to this supper should be happy. We are being given a mission worthy of our lives.

"Lord, I am not worthy" to be sent on this mission, we say, "but only say the word, and I shall be healed"—and ready to be sent forth.

As we file up for Communion, we are each told, "the Body of Christ." It is kind of an ambiguous statement. In fact, we used to be told, "This is the Body of Christ," but now the eucharistic minister says only, "the Body of Christ" or "the Blood of Christ." From the point of view of the Dismissal this is significant. When we eat the flesh and blood of Jesus, we *become* the body and blood of Christ to the world. We are going out into the world to continue *his* mission to inaugurated the kingdom of God.

And so we say, "Amen," or "So be it." We are accepting that mission once again. We are ready to go.

• • •

The priest reads one last prayer after Communion that gets us ready for the Dismissal. For example, on the Twenty-fifth Sunday in Ordinary Time he says, "Lord, help us with your kindness. Make us strong through the Eucharist. May we put into action the saving mystery we celebrate. We ask this in the name of Jesus the Lord." And we all say, "Amen." We're ready to go. We all stand up.

The priest gives us a final blessing, and then the priest or deacon sends us forth: "Go in peace to love and serve the Lord," he says. "Thanks be to God," we respond.

If the Mass has been done with the Dismissal in mind, we will all understand what is happening. We are being sent forth "in peace"—the peace of Jesus, not the peace that the world gives—to "love and serve the Lord." The Lord Jesus wants only one thing from those who love and serve him. He wants us to continue his mission, the same one he carried out himself, the same one he sent his original disciples on. "To love and serve the Lord" means to help bring about the kingdom of God "on earth as it is in heaven." We are to be the body and blood of Christ in the world. It is truly a mission worthy of our lives, and we are as prepared as we will ever be to do it. And so we say, "Thanks be to God," not because the Mass has ended, but because it has just begun.

A Story about the Dismissal

. . . .

"Go in peace to love and serve the Lord," the presider said.

"Thanks be to God," the congregation responded and prepared to leave.

"But remember," the presider continued. "Love is patient, love is kind. Love is not envious nor boastful nor arrogant nor rude. Love does not insist on its own way. Love is neither irritable nor resentful. It does not rejoice in wrongdoing but only rejoices in the truth. Love bears all things, believes all things, hopes all things, endures all things. Love never ends.

"So once again I say, Let us go to practice love."

"In that case, Lord, have mercy on us," responded the congregation.

Questions for Reflection and Discussion

....

1. Do you think it is our actions or God's that will bring about the kingdom of God "on earth as it is in heaven"? Explain your answer.

2. If you actually become Jesus, how will you act differently once you leave the church? How will you act differently at work? How will you act differently at home and with your friends? How will you act differently in your community and civic affairs?

3. Are you ready to be sent forth on the greatest mission ever devised? Why or why not? What will it take to convince you and prepare you to take it on?

part three

The Spirituality
of Work

· ·

nine

···

Sustaining the Sending
Forth

··

LET'S IMAGINE YOU have been sent forth from Mass, shot like a cannonball back into your daily life to carry out an impossible mission given to you by Jesus himself. How are you going to do it, and what is going to sustain you until the next time you can return to Mass? You are going to do it through your daily work, and what will sustain you is the spirituality of work.

The first thing that needs to be said is that you are already practicing the spirituality of work. You might not call it that, and you might not even be aware that you are doing it, but every time you do a good job at something, every time you think about others as well as yourself, every time you make the world a little better place, you are practicing the spirituality of work.

So don't make too big a deal about it. The spirituality of work is not brain surgery. It is not even as hard, for example, as practicing Zen Buddhism or Transcendental Meditation. It is certainly not as hard as going to Mass or saying the rosary daily. In a lot of ways, the spirituality of work is the most common sense of all the spiritualities. It is certainly the most accessible to the average person, because every one of us works.

That's right, everyone works, even the retired and the unemployed. Parents work at raising children; spouses work at staying committed and in love. The dying work, as do those who are giving birth or being born. Sometimes we are paid for our work; often we are not—at least monetarily. In fact, one of the worst things to happen to a person is to be without work to do. (Just ask someone who is incarcerated or involuntarily unemployed and is not allowed to work, or someone who is paralyzed either physically or emotionally and cannot work.)

Yet the experience of human beings regarding work is a mixed bag indeed. A few people love every bit of the work they do, and they love it all the time. Others hate almost all the work they do almost all the time. Most of us are somewhere in the middle—liking some of our work or at least some aspects of it, and disliking or being indifferent to the rest.

Some of our work is physically, emotionally, psychologically, or even spiritually exhausting. Other work we do is invigorating or gratifying or fulfilling in some way. Some work has obvious social value—nursing, garbage collecting, parenting, for example. Other work is morally neutral or even objectionable on the face of it. A lot of work is boring. Some of it is difficult, sometimes even dangerous or bad for our health.

Other times, our work is so easy and natural it can seem like cutting soft butter. It flows from who we are and what we like to do. It just happens, and we almost don't realize we have been working. When Ernie Banks offered, "Let's play two," he meant it, and sometimes we mean it, too.

What are we to make of the mixed bag that is work? Not much. We aren't going to change the nature of work, nor are we all going to find the perfect work to do all the time. What we can do is change how we approach our work, how we do our work, how we experience the divine present in our work-aday world.

. . .

What do I mean when I say you are already practicing the spirituality of work? I mean that since we all work, and since most of us experience work as a mixed bag, we all have to make spiritual decisions about our work. When you do that, you are practicing the spirituality of work, whether you call it that or not, whether you realize you are doing so or not.

First of all, whether you are caring for an aging spouse or parent round the clock for free, or running an international conglomerate for lots of money, your work has meaning. It has meaning because you assign it meaning, and the process of assigning meaning to your work is a spiritual task.

For some of us, the meaning is simple: We work to make a living. There is nothing wrong with this meaning; it fits with the Genesis story that we must work by the sweat of our brow. It is a good thing to make a living, to "put bread on the table," to "feed the family" and "put a roof over their heads." Consider the alternative. The world's economic engine would not continue to run without this meaning of work. In fact, we have seen during the Great Depression and at other times and places what happens when this purpose and meaning of work is ignored or denigrated. Even Saint Paul said, "We also gave you the rule that if you don't work, you don't eat" (2 Thes 3:10), and then he showed by working as a tentmaker that he meant business.

But making a living is not the only meaning of work. For one thing, we all do work for which we don't get paid: around the home, in the community, at church, in politics, with our children. Some people volunteer or are underpaid for what they do, but their work still has meaning. Others are fairly paid or even overpaid, but their work has meaning beyond the money.

To the extent that we seek to discover or assign meaning to our work, then, we are practicing the spirituality of work. Some people find meaning in producing or providing quality goods and services. Others see work as more of a duty or obligation, one that they fulfill sometimes willingly and sometimes reluctantly, but always competently and reliably. Still others see work as a partnership with God in the ongoing creation of the universe. They see that the job of bringing order out of chaos is not yet complete and that, for whatever reason, God is using the work of human hands, bodies, minds, and spirits to finish the job.

This "search for meaning," as Victor Frankel called it, differentiates us from the other animals. It is the first step in the practice of the spirituality of work, and it is one that all those who work—including you—take at some point.

· · ·

There are other questions that you must answer about your work, and each of them eventually leads to a practice of the spirituality of work. We must all decide, for example, how we are going to treat others at work. Virtually everyone who works has others they must deal with: colleagues, employees, bosses, customers, clients, suppliers, delivery people, even competitors. How we decide to treat others at work is a spiritual matter, even if we don't think of it that way. For example, will we give an eye for an eye, or will we turn the other cheek? Or, more likely, will it be sometimes the one and sometimes the other and most often something in between?

How will we decide which it will be in any given situation? This is a spiritual question.

Another question we must all answer is how we are going to decide right from wrong at work. Does it depend on whether or not we are likely to be caught, the circumstance each time, how we feel that day, or what others are doing or not doing? This is another spiritual question, and we all have to answer it—at least by our actions.

Likewise, we must decide how we are going to balance our work with our other needs and obligations. What about our need for personal time and leisure? How about our obligations to friends, family, church, and community? Again, we do make decisions on how to balance our responsibilities, and those decisions are spiritual—whether we admit it or not.

So you see, you are already practicing the spirituality of work. The real question is how well you are practicing it and how you might improve your practice of it.

A Story about Work

You go to work one day and discover God standing there waiting for you. "Hey, God," you say. "Where have you been?"

"I've been here all the time," God insists, "waiting for you to notice me."

"Okay, okay," you say. "So now that I know you're here, what do I do now?"

"*We* get to work," God answers matter-of-factly.

Questions for Reflection and Discussion

1. Take a sheet of paper and draw a line down the middle. On one side list all the things you like about the various kinds of work you do. On the other side list all the things you don't like. On which side do you find God? Explain.

2. What are the various meanings you find in your work? Give an example of a time recently when you experienced each of the meanings.

3. Describe how you try to treat others at work. How do you decide what is right or wrong at work? How successful are you at balancing your work with the rest of your life? Why?

ten

....

God and Work

....

GOD WORKS. IN the Judeo-Christian tradition, almost nothing is clearer than this. Just open the Bible to page one and you'll read: "In the beginning, God created the heavens and the earth" (Gn 1:1). A little later in the first chapter of Genesis it says, "By the seventh day God had finished his work, and so he rested" (Gn 2:2).

Notice that God only *rested* from work on that first Sabbath. Presumably, God was right back at work the next morning. Later, in the gospel of John, Jesus makes it clear that God continues to work: "My Father has never stopped working, and that is why I keep on working" (Jn 5:17).

What are the implications of God's work for our spirituality? First of all, it makes it almost impossible not to view work as something holy. If God does it, by definition work must be good and sacred in some very real, very basic way.

Second, if God's work is ongoing, then our work must be connected to it, just as Jesus' was. When you think about it, it is primarily through the work of human beings that God continues the ongoing creation of the universe. For better or worse, God succeeds to the extent that we do—or do not do— our work with competence, compassion, and creativity.

Third, if our work is connected with God's work, then there are not two categories of work—one sacred and holy, and the other secular and meaningless. This eliminates the classic distinction between religious work, which is often character- ized as "ministry" or "vocation," and the non-church-related work of most laypeople on their jobs, with their families, and in their volunteer civic organizations. What makes work holy is that it is apparently God's intention for us. This means that it is not so much what we do as how we do it and why we do it that gives ultimate meaning to our work.

Finally, in the Abrahamic tradition it is not just a coinci- dence that we happen to do the same activity as God (i.e., work). We work precisely *because* we are made in the image of God. God works, and since we are to be like God, we work as well. In the very act of working, we share in the divine life. This is why we can be sure that God is always present when we are working, whether we realize it or not.

• • •

At this point, you might be saying, "Wait a minute; this is not my experience of work. I don't notice God in my work- place all that often, and my work doesn't seem to be making the world much of a better place." And you might be right. For most of us, work is not a walk in the park. Often our work is difficult, unfulfilling, exhausting, even dangerous or mean- ingless. How can it also be spiritual?

The Bible, the same place we get our view of God as a worker, also holds the key to understanding why work so often seems to be a burden to be borne rather than produc- tive activity to be embraced. In trying to explain the human condition, the writers of scripture struggled to understand how things got so messed up from God's plan, and they concluded that sin is the answer. So while the human originally gets put into the Garden of Eden "to take care of it and to look after it" (Gn 2:15), after the fall women will "suffer terribly" when they give birth and men "will have to sweat to earn a living" (see Gn 3:16-19).

So there it is. At one point work is free and easy, connected with God's work and without pain and sweat. Then we humans sin and work turns into a curse. Which is it? Is our work our participation in God's ongoing creation of the universe, or is our work the punishment for the sin of our first parents?

Our own experience probably provides the best answer. Sometimes when we work, we feel ourselves running on all cylinders—efficient, effective, engaged. Other times we feel harried, unproductive, put upon. Take the work of parenting, for example. There is not a parent who will not tell you that sometimes parenting can be the greatest experience in the world, even when it is difficult. Other times, however, parenting can be a frustrating, frightening, even maddening endeavor. What causes the difference? It is how in tune our parenting is with God's way of doing things. When we are aligned with the divine way of work, we are in the pre-Fall garden, where all work is spiritual. As we allow ourselves to wander from the way God would have things, we find ourselves unhappy, unfulfilled, and unproductive. So the oppression of work is not so much a punishment for our sins as it is a result of not working in the spirit for which we were designed.

· · ·

The spirituality of work has nothing to do with how easy or hard the work is. My wife Kathy likes to garden, and she sweats a lot when she does. When I watch her digging up plants and moving them around and carrying stones to make a pathway, it looks like hard work to me. But when Kathy is working on her garden, she is in the presence of God in a way that I really can't comprehend.

I, on the other hand, love to write. I am writing this book right now, and I feel the hand of God on my shoulder. That does not mean that it is not difficult or that I don't get frustrated or that I don't have trouble balancing my writing with my other obligations. It just means that my writing work is more like "tending the garden" than it is working by "the sweat of my brow."

What do we tell a woman who is going through childbirth? "You're doing a great job! Keep up the good work!" God knows that it is painful, but the woman also knows that what she is doing is fulfilling God's work of creation.

So, our experience is that work is important, meaningful, and God-like, and also that it is hard, tiring, and frustrating. Sometimes it is more one way, sometimes it is more the other. The spirituality of work can be practiced in either case.

Walter Cronkite, the venerable television reporter, anchorman, and commentator, feels that the one date from our age that will be remembered five hundred years from now is July 20, 1969. That is, of course, the day that a human being first walked on the moon. Cronkite believes that by the year 2469, humans will be living on other planets and will remember July 20, 1969, as the day that humankind broke away from being tied to the Earth. If so, then it will have certainly been, as Neil Armstrong said, "One small step for man, one giant step for mankind."

Whether you share Cronkite's belief is not the point. Just imagine for a moment that he is correct, that someday we might be living on other planets. It might even be that we had polluted Earth so badly that people could not live here at all. If that scenario were to occur, we would have to accept that it was "God's will." But we would also have to admit that it was brought about by the work of human hands, minds, and spirits. We would have gotten to the other planets through our creativity and intelligence and good work, but we would also have destroyed our planet through our selfishness and stupidity and bad work.

Thus it is with God and our work. We are either on the same page, pulling in the same direction, trying to ascertain and then do God's will in our daily lives, or we are opposing the divine spirit, trying to do things our way, worrying only about our self-interest in the narrowest of terms. The spirituality of work is a spirituality that tries to keep us aware of the presence of God and allow that awareness to influence how we do our work. With the spirituality of work, we can conquer the stars. Without it, we can destroy our very nest.

A Story about God at Work

A woman went into a marketplace, looked around, and saw a sign that read "God's Fruit Market."

"Thank goodness. It's about time," the woman said to herself.

She went inside and said, "I would like a perfect banana, a perfect cantaloupe, a perfect strawberry, and a perfect peach."

God, who was behind the counter, shrugged and said, "I'm sorry, Madam, I sell only seeds."

Questions for Reflection or Discussion

1. Name one time you experienced the presence of God in your work (paid or unpaid). What did it feel like? How did it affect your work? What happens when you try to repeat that experience?

2. If you were God, how would you view the quality of the work you presently do? Would you be proud, embarrassed, understanding, apologetic, enthusiastic? Why would you feel that way?

3. Find one story or passage in the Bible that speaks to you about God's work. Read it. Reflect on it. Apply it to your own work. If you have the time, type or write out the passage and post it somewhere in your workplace.

eleven

....

Jesus and Work

....

I WAS ONCE asked to give a retreat to a group of businesspeople. After I had accepted, they told me that they wanted a "Jesus-centered retreat" on the spirituality of work. I objected that I didn't think I could do so.

I had never really thought much about Jesus as a worker. I grew up with the idea that Jesus was the son of a carpenter and most likely worked as a carpenter himself, but there is really not much in scripture about that—almost as if it wasn't important what he did before his public ministry.

Instead, Jesus is presented as a wandering preacher with no visible means of support. He even complains that he "doesn't have a place to call his own" (Lk 9:58), and his public ministry is supported by donations from wealthy women, including Mary of Magdala (see Lk 21:3).

What's worse, Jesus seems to put down ordinary jobs in favor of becoming full-time missionaries. He tells Peter and Andrew that they should leave their fishing boat and nets and come with him: "I will teach you how to bring in people instead of fish" (Mt 4:19). He takes Matthew away from his job collecting taxes (see Mt 9:9). He tells a rich and important man to "go and sell everything you own," presumably give up his job, and "come and be my follower" (see Lk 18:22). Finally, some of the parables that Jesus tells seem totally out of touch with the world of work. Does he really think that people hired at five in the afternoon should be paid as much as those who worked all day (Mt 20:1-16)? What about the corrupt steward that Jesus seems to praise for selling out his master to his debtors (Lk 16:1-13)? Even Jesus' marriage and family advice seems suspect. Should parents really give their kids their share of the family fortune when they ask (Lk 15:11-32)? Is lust in the heart truly as serious as adultery (Mt 5:28)?

I just didn't think that Jesus was a good role model for workers or that his advice on daily life was all that practical. How could I run a "Jesus-centered" retreat on the spirituality of work? I was about to tell the group that I couldn't facilitate their retreat.

. . .

As I was preparing to call them, however, I read an opinion piece in the *Chicago Tribune* about what makes a person a genius. The author quoted Albert Einstein as saying that genius was the ability to hold two contradictory ideas in your mind at the same time. That seems to make sense. Then, for some reason, I thought about my businesspeople's retreat. It struck me that if Jesus was a genius (which I firmly believe he was), then he would have had this ability. I wondered what some of the contradictory ideas were that Jesus held in his mind at one time. Once I started thinking that way, of course, many things came to mind: life and death, loving our enemies, sickness and healing, power and weakness, etc.

When I applied this idea to the spirituality of work, one contradiction that Jesus seemed to embrace was this: We have never done enough; we have already done enough. As I flipped through the gospels, this idea seemed to jump out at me. When the rich and important man thought he had done enough, Jesus was quick to challenge him to do much more, but when the woman caught in adultery was feeling that she was a complete failure, Jesus basically told her that her regret was enough.

Over and over, Jesus seemed to take great delight in challenging those who thought they were doing enough (e.g., the Pharisees, the disciples) to do more, while at the same time assuring those who thought they had not done enough (e.g., sinners, tax collectors, those suffering from disease) that they had already done enough, that all they had to do was "believe" and they would be healed.

Think you've done enough, Nicodemus? You must be born again.

Think you haven't done enough, woman at the well? I am living water; all you've got to do is ask for it.

Want to be first in heaven, James and John? Be the last.

Want to follow me, Andrew? Just come and see where I live (unless you think you've already done enough, in which case you have to give up everything).

The Good Samaritan? He's already done enough. So has the man born blind, the leper who returned to give thanks, the woman who touched Jesus' cloak, the official whose son was sick, and on and on.

But Judas? You think you've given up a lot? The sacrifices you will be asked to make will prove too much for you.

Peter, Thomas, James, John—the minute you think you've proven yourself and are in line for a big pat on the back, watch out.

Pilate, you weak man, you are not off the hook just because you show Jesus a little compassion. You've got to take on the chief priests and the angry crowds if you want to be saved.

Gregory, you think you haven't done enough when you finish a hard day's work as a businessman, writer, husband, father, friend, neighbor, homeowner, citizen, parishioner? You have. But at the same time, Gregory, wasn't there something more you could have done if you had been a little more aware of the importance of your work, a little more in tune with what God wants you to do in your daily life? Of course there was.

• • •

I called up the organizers of the business group and said I thought I could do their Jesus-centered retreat on the spirituality of work. The theme would be that at the exact same time in the workplace—not sometimes one way and sometimes the other, but at the exact same time—we have never done enough and we have already done enough. It would be at the vortex of this contradiction that we would discover the spirituality of our work.

I spent three days with a group of businesspeople from the Hartford, Connecticut, area, and we explored this idea based on our own experience in the workplace. We used the scriptures, and especially the parables of Jesus, to see how we might do our work knowing that we have never done enough and yet have already done enough.

For example, our workplaces should be like the kingdom of God, but we know that they are not. No problem, Jesus would say, the kingdom has already begun; it is within you, but it won't finally arrive for a long time. It's like a mustard seed, or a pearl of great price, or a man who went out to sow. Don't worry so much about it, Jesus would say. Be like the birds of the air or the lilies of the field. *They* don't do "enough," but the Father takes care of them anyway.

But don't be like the man who built his house on sand or the Pharisee who congratulated himself in the Temple. Be like the widow who bugged the judge for justice or the woman who scoured her house until she found the coin that she had lost. (And even then she hadn't done enough until she called in her friends to rejoice with her that what she had lost was found.)

And if your prodigal son messes up and spends all his money, you've still got to welcome him back and kill the fatted calf for him. Don't be like the brother who thought he had done enough just because he was faithful and honest and hardworking.

What has all this got to do with the spirituality of work? It is a way of thinking about it. Virtually everyone who works has the experience that sometimes work can be very good and productive, even loving and holy. Right then is where Jesus will step in and say, "Be careful, there is a lot more to do, you have not yet done enough." But there are other times when work makes us tired, discouraged, angry, even alienated from God, ourselves, and others. Jesus is there, too, to remind us that in his eyes, at least, we have already done enough.

When we can do our work on the edge, at the intersection of these two truths, at the place where *at one and the same time* we know that we have already done enough and we have not yet done enough, *then and only then* will we be living a Christ-centered spirituality of work.

A Story about Jesus and Work

Jesus and Peter were walking down the road together when they came upon a man who had been set upon by robbers and left to die.

"We've got to help the poor man," Peter said to the Lord as he began to crawl down into the ditch where the man lay.

"Don't worry about it, Peter," Jesus said. "There's a Samaritan businessman right behind us who will take care of him."

"OK," Peter said as he crawled back out of the ditch. "But I don't understand why we should let a Samaritan do a *mitzva* for one of our fellow Jews."

"Ah, but we do a *mitzva* for the businessman by buying some of his oil and wine," said Jesus.

Questions for Reflection or Discussion

1. Which do you feel more often in your work: that you have already done enough or that you have not yet done enough? Reflect on the fact that Jesus would say that you are wrong. Can you live with the tension of constantly feeling that you should be doing more and accepting the fact that you are already doing all you can?

2. Take one of the following three parables of Jesus—Workers in a Vineyard (Mt 20:1-16), A Dishonest Manager (Lk 16:1-13), or Two Sons (Lk 15:11-32)—and reflect on it from the contradiction of already having done enough and never having done enough.

3. Have an imaginary conversation with Jesus about your work. What would you tell him about what you do? What

might he say if you started complaining about it? What if you started bragging about it?

twelve

....

The Church and Work

....

WHEN COMEDIAN CHEVY Chase was on *Saturday Night Live,* he had a signature line that always drew a laugh: "I'm Chevy Chase, and you're not." Stupid as it was, this statement carried with it a deep lesson for the spirituality of work. I call it the "Chevy Chase Syndrome."

Here is how it works. People who have a high opinion of themselves or the importance of the work they do often communicate to others that "My work is spiritual, and yours is not." Nowhere is this Chevy Chase Syndrome more prevalent than in church circles: "I have a vocation, and you don't"; "My work is ministry, and yours isn't"; "I have been called to do my work, and you haven't." Not only is church ministerial work held up as being especially holy, but often the ordinary work of others is dismissed as being somehow tainted or unimportant: "He's just a janitor." "She makes big bucks as a lawyer." "I don't know what they do."

Even more frustrating is the self-righteousness of some religious writers and even saints about the superiority of their particular brand of spirituality. For example, Trappist monk Thomas Keating has been quoted as saying, "Silence is the language of God; all else is poor translation." Now that may very well be Father Keating's experience, but it is also a patently self-serving statement for someone who has taken the vow of silence. In fact, my own experience is that God speaks at least equally well in the music of Beethoven or in some of the conversations I have had with my wife and children. No less an authority than the gospel of John says, "In the beginning was . . . the Word" (Jn 1:1), not the silence.

So in some ways, the spirituality of work does not have strong tradition or support in church circles (although I will try to correct that impression in the next chapter by exploring some of the saints and movements that have been supportive of work). But what is definitely true is that the church has been and continues to be ambivalent about work and the spirituality of work.

• • •

In the early church there was the movement by the desert fathers and others to get as far away as possible from the world and to live as simply as possible. Work was seen as a necessity at best, but the focus was clearly on prayer and meditation as the keys to the spiritual life.

Later, Saint Benedict and others reformed the monastic movement and made work more central to the life of the monks. "Ora et labora," Benedict taught them, "Prayer and work." But still, the monastic life was seen as spiritually superior to life in the world, and contemplative spirituality was seen as the best or even the only spirituality. (Shades of Chevy Chase.)

Certainly, the Christian tradition had its advocates for the work of laypeople in the world, going all the way back to Jesus himself, who picked fishermen and tax collectors and housewives and other ordinary workers as his disciples. Maybe Jesus himself was a carpenter; certainly his father was. Some of the greatest saints in Christian history were advocates of the spirituality of the work of daily life, including Ignatius Loyola, Francis and Clare of Assisi, Theresa the Little Flower, Francis de Sales, and Jane Frances de Chantal. Although there are not many lay Catholic saints who were canonized primarily for their secular work, Thomas More was a lawyer and politician, Martin of Tours was a soldier, Joseph was a carpenter, Elizabeth of Hungary was a queen, Don Bosco was a student, and Isidore was a farmer. It's not so much that the list of saints is small as it is unknown. Certainly, there are millions of Christians who have lived out their lives in fidelity to their faith, practicing a spirituality of the work they have done. But they are not "Chevy Chase" because they are not famous and have not been held up as models of sanctity. You know who they are in your own lives, and so do I.

. . .

The bigger problem with the church and work is what is said about work day after day in our liturgies, our religious education, our sacramental preparation, our parochial schools, and our religious books and resources. What is being communicated is that work isn't all that important to the Christian life, or that if it is, we don't know what to do or say about it.

Be honest: What is the definition of a good, vibrant parish or congregation? Isn't it the parish that experiences good liturgies and homilies and music, provides hospitality to strangers, shares resources with others, and especially has lots and lots of parish ministries and lay ministers? None of this is bad stuff, of course, but aren't these activities—in fact, isn't the church itself—a means to a greater end? And isn't that end our mission to help bring about the kingdom or reign of God "on earth as it is in heaven," as we pray each day in the Lord's Prayer?

The primary way we carry out that mission is through our work. "My Father has never stopped working; and that is why I keep on working," Jesus said (Jn 5:17). And we, who are now the body of Christ in the world, work as well. What we need from the church is not "I'm Chevy Chase, and you're not." What we need from the church is to be sent forth on a mission worthy of our lives, equipped with a spirituality that will challenge and sustain us in the midst of the inevitable hustle and bustle, ups and downs, joys and disappointments of our workday.

How can that happen? It can happen if the church can develop and train people in the spirituality of work. If we get the Dismissal from Mass right, we will get the mission right. And if we get the mission right, we will get the spirituality right. And if we get the spirituality right, we will accomplish the mission.

A Story about Respect

The abbot and a new monk were invited to the home of a family near the monastery. Honored to have such distinguished guests, the family put on a great feast.

But the younger monk was fasting, so he ate only a few sticks of celery.

On the way back to the abbey, the abbot said to the young monk: "The next time, fast from your presumption."

Questions for Reflection or Discussion

....

1. Name a saint—canonized or not—whose work in the world you admire. What is it about that person's work that draws your attention?

2. Find your favorite biblical passage or church document about work. Reread it aloud. List three points about it that you want to remember in your own work.

3. Describe how your parish or congregation sends you forth into the world of work. Do you feel equipped to carry out your mission with a spirituality of work? Why or why not?

thirteen

....

The Christian Spiritual Tradition

....

LET'S NOT PRETEND we are reinventing the wheel here. Work is such an integral part of the human experience that all religious traditions take it seriously, including the Christian tradition. Sometimes work is viewed as a burden, some kind of punishment for sins of ourselves or our forebears. Other times work is considered an unfortunate necessity, something that must be done to meet our material needs but certainly nothing holy or sacred or even important on a spiritual level. Still other times, work is seen as some sort of ascetic practice, something to clear the mind or offer to God as a gift.

None of these positions give much dignity to work or to the worker. Fortunately, in the Christian tradition (as well as in many other religions), there is also a strain of very good theory and practice on the spirituality of work. Sometimes you just have to dig a little bit for it.

Let's divide our search into three categories: scriptural views of the spirituality of work, church movements' views of the spirituality of work, and modern views of the spirituality of work. We will, of course, only be able to summarize and hit some of the highlights, and I apologize in advance for oversimplifying and for my own lack of knowledge on these issues. I do encourage people who are so inclined to do more research on the spirituality of work in all the religions, especially the Christian and even more specifically the Catholic traditions. I have a feeling that it is there even more strongly than I am aware, but the very fact that it is not well known to us kind of proves my point.

. . .

The best single resource I know on work in the scriptures is the *Word in Life Bible,* which has more than 250 short articles and commentary under "work" alone, including on the nature and value of work, people at work, the believer's "work style," career changes and planning, communicating the gospel in the workplace, competition and conflict, decision making and planning, honesty and integrity, money and profits, success and significance, supervisors and subordinates, work and the church, work and the environment, work and leisure, and models for marketplace Christians. So the idea that the Bible doesn't deal with work is dead wrong. In fact, we would only be surprised if the Bible didn't deal with work, because work is such a vital component of the human experience. But if we were to summarize what the scriptures say about work, it would be this:

Work is good. Even though it appears that work is the punishment for Adam and Eve's "original" sin, it is clear that God works (and so work is good) and that our work is a participation in God's work.

Jesus worked. We assume he worked as a carpenter, like Joseph, until he was about thirty. But even if that is not true, we know for certain that he worked during his public life and that many of his parables and stories were about people's work. "The Father has never stopped working," he said, "and that is why I keep on working" (Jn 5:17).

We are supposed to work. Paul said, "If you don't work, you don't eat" (2 Thes 3:10), and he showed by his own example (see Acts 18:3) that work has its own dignity.

The primary work of all Christians is to help bring about the kingdom of God on earth as it is in heaven. This is not a specialized job for those who work for the church. It is the mission that all Christians are sent on by virtue of their baptism and confirmation, and it is carried out primarily in our daily lives in our jobs, with our families, and in our community activities. As Jesus prayed to the Father, "I am sending them into the world, just as you sent me" (Jn 17:18).

. . .

As the church developed over the centuries, there have been many movements that sought to combine spirituality and work. These took many forms:

In the monastic tradition, Benedict, Bernard, Teresa of Avila, Therese of Lisieux, and others sought to make work part of daily prayer. *"Ora et Labora"* — "Prayer and Work"—is still one of the mottos of the Benedictines. This view was aimed primarily at the monks themselves, but it filtered into the lives of the laypeople who surrounded the monasteries. One of the classic works on the spirituality of work is *The Practice of the Presence of God* by Brother Lawrence, a medieval monk.

Over the centuries the great non-monastic religious orders, such as the Augustinians, the Franciscans, the Jesuits, the Dominicans, the Salesians, the Sisters of Mercy, the Sisters of St. Joseph, the Cabrini Sisters and others, and more recently lay movements such as *Cursillo, Focolare,* and even *Opus Dei,* and many of the "third orders" and "lay associates" have all sought to explore the spirituality of work. Many of these orders and movements started out aimed at laypeople in regular jobs, but eventually became clericalized and internally-oriented themselves. Still, they have kept alive the idea that work in the world is the primary place where most laypeople live out their spirituality and mission.

The Protestant Reformation, with its emphasis on the importance of the laity in the church, also made many contributions to the spirituality of work. Luther's idea of "the priesthood of all believers," which taught that every person has a call from God, is still an important part of Protestant thought. More recently, through the work of people like Episcopalian Mark Gibbs, Lutherans William Diehl and Sally Simmel, and Intervarsity Christian Fellowship's Peter Hammond, there has been a strong movement of what many Protestants call "ministry in daily life," which focuses on the mission of every Christian in his or her daily work.

Catholic social teaching over the last hundred years or so has also made important contributions to the spirituality of work. Papal encyclicals, such as Pope Leo XIII's *Rerum Novarum* and Pope John Paul II's *On Human Work,* have raised the idea of the spiritual importance of work and the dignity of the worker. The publication in 1977 of *The Chicago Declaration of Christian Concern* by a group of lay leaders and clergy—including Ed Marciniak, Russ Barta, and Msgr. Daniel Cantwell—led to the development of the National Center for the Laity, which, under the leadership of my friend and collaborator, William Droel, has been the primary Catholic proponent in the United States of the idea that the laity's role is primarily "in and to the world," and that the spirituality of work is a real spirituality that can be and is being practiced in the midst of the hustle and bustle of daily life.

. . .

In the last ten years, there has been a virtual explosion of study about the spirituality of work. Some of this research has been fueled by interest in academic circles about the phenomenon at such places as Yale University, St. Thomas University, the University of San Diego, DePaul University, and other places.

Another strong source of interest has been among evangelical Protestants and Catholics. There are now a variety of organizations with names like "Christ in the workplace" and "marketplace ministries." Some of these efforts, unfortunately, have been aimed almost exclusively at top-level business and professional managers, as if these are the only workers who need or can practice a spirituality of work.

Another group that is studying this issue is comprised of Catholic institutions such as hospitals, colleges, and social service agencies. Since their Catholic identity is no longer derived from the fact that they are run by full-time religious priests, sisters, or brothers, they are investigating the idea of the spirituality of work as a possible answer to the question, "What makes this institution Catholic or Christian?" The answer might be, "It is in the way we go about our work and the ultimate goal of what we are trying to accomplish."

There are now a plethora of books out on the spirituality of work. While they vary greatly in quality, they all are breaking new ground in exploring exactly what a spirituality of work might look like. Likewise, there are newsletters, magazines, and especially websites that now focus almost exclusively on spirituality and work. Even the secular media has gotten into the act. *Fortune* magazine ran a cover story not too long ago titled "God and Business: The Search for Spirituality in the Workplace," and this has been followed by articles in other major periodicals and newspapers. I myself maintain a free e-mail list of over a thousand people on this issue, which you are welcome to join at any time by sending me an e-mail at spiritualitywork@aol.com.

So the spirituality of work is no longer looked upon as an oxymoron. It may, however, be a fad. What will prevent this, of course, is if it truly joins the mainstream of Christian thought and practice. This will happen when it starts being practiced by lay Christians in ordinary secular jobs—by people like you and those in your parishes and congregations.

A Story about the Saints

God called a meeting of all the great saints. Everyone was there.

"We've got a problem," Peter announced. "A lot of people are coming to heaven expecting to never have to work again."

"Where did they get that idea?" said Mother Teresa. "It wouldn't be heaven if we didn't have any work to do."

"Do you tell them about the three weeks paid vacation?" Francis of Assisi asked.

"And of course they all get their feast day off, canonized or not!" said Kateri Tekakwitha.

Everyone laughed, including God.

Questions for Reflection or Discussion

1. Name three saints who were either not priests, bishops, or popes; a founder or member of a religious order; a martyr; a king or queen; or someone who took the vow of celibacy.

If you can't think of three, name three people from your own experience whom you consider to be saints.

2. What is your favorite story about work from the Bible? Why? If you don't have one, start looking. (It won't take you long to find one.)

3. Of all the things in the Christian tradition, which do you find the most helpful as you think about practicing the spirituality of work? Why?

fourteen

....

Getting into the World

....

IF YOU ARE like most people, your ideas about spirituality were formed by both your religious training and the popular culture. What both of these disparate sources have in common is that they tend to portray spirituality as somehow set apart from the world—especially the world of work.

Popular culture (TV, movies, literature, news, even comic strips) tends to view spirituality as something cute, quaint, and mostly irrelevant to people's daily lives. Most of these are harmless enough. They are either so far out as to be non-threatening (such as *Buffy the Vampire Slayer*, *Ghost Whisperer*, or *Joan of Arcadia*) or they are so sweet and syrupy that no one could mistake them for real life (such as *Seventh Heaven*). Television shows and movies that purport to show real people dealing with real issues from a religious or spiritual viewpoint seem to be able to do so only if one or more of the major characters are priests, ministers, nuns, or at least mystics of some sort.

Think about it. Do you really know the spiritual views of the people on *Friends* or *Seinfeld* or *Survivor?* How about Jimmy Stewart's character in *It's a Wonderful Life* or Gregory Peck's in *To Kill a Mockingbird?* Do any of John Grisham's characters go to church or allow their spirituality to infuse their actions?

One of the most popular comic strips in recent years has been *Dilbert,* which is really a one-joke cartoon. The joke is that work is hell and that there is zero spirituality in the workplace. Actually, one of the popular shows that *has* dealt with religion and spirituality over the years is *The Simpsons,* although the portrayal of most church-going folk is none too flattering.

And when the news tries to cover religion, it seems that it can only focus on the controversial (abortion, gay marriage, euthanasia), the bizarre (Mary's face on a grilled cheese sandwich), or the other-worldly (apparitions, miracles, near-death experiences). When *Fortune* magazine ran their cover story on spirituality in the workplace a few years ago, the only cover image they could come up with was the sun breaking through clouds. When the media wants to cover "spirituality," they often head for the nearest monastery—or at least rectory, parsonage, or chancery office.

The bottom line is that you could wander through popular culture and never get the impression that religion and spirituality is important in most people's lives at all. The same, by the way, is true of the media's depiction of work. Unless he or she is a doctor, lawyer, cop, or schoolteacher, a character's work is usually irrelevant to the plot. So when we come to explore the spirituality of work in popular culture, the pickings are slim indeed.

• • •

Organized religion doesn't do much better in its depiction of spirituality and work. Most books on spirituality push one version or another of a "get away from the world, at least for a while" approach that has its roots in monastic contemplative spirituality and a spirituality practiced by religious professionals who do this sort of thing for a living. (Truth in advertising: I make my living publishing books on spirituality and religion, so I should be suspect here as well; however, my own spiritual search has primarily been about finding God in my daily work on my job, with my family, and in my community activities. I have never been especially interested in or good at "finding God" by getting away from the hustle and bustle of my daily life.)

How about you? How and where do you practice your spirituality? Silence, solitude, and simplicity are the hallmarks of most spiritual practice, whereas noise, crowds, and complexity are the realities of most lay people. Are the laity to say that we are mere amateurs in the spirituality game and throw up our hands in frustration that we can never achieve holiness? Or can we look for ways to raise our awareness of the presence of God in the midst of our daily lives and allow that awareness to sanctify everything that we do?

There is nothing wrong with contemplative spirituality, of course, unless it is proposed as the best or the only spirituality. Jesus' admonition of Martha, "Mary has chosen what is best, and it will not be taken away from her" (Lk 10:42), has always been taken as proof of the superiority of contemplative spirituality over a more active spirituality, such as the spirituality of work. We forget, however, that Jesus loved Martha, busy as she was, and it was Martha—the "type A" personality and workaholic *par excellence*—who finally recognized Jesus for who he really was: "I believe that you are Christ, the Son of God. You are the one we hoped would come into the world" (Jn 11:27).

Much of Christian spirituality, especially in the Catholic tradition, has been "other worldly." We Catholics love our candles and stained glass and incense and sacred music and vestments, but if we aren't careful, it isn't much of a leap to equate spirituality with those accoutrements, when the real stuff of spirituality lies right at our fingertips each day.

. . .

Spirituality is a lot simpler than most of us have been led to believe. In fact, the hardest part of spirituality is remembering to be spiritual! If we remember, we tend to do it, because we humans are spiritual beings just as much as we are physical, psychological, emotional, and intellectual beings. But we often forget this when we are caught up in the chaos of daily life. Perhaps this is why contemplative spirituality is so popular and attractive. It is easy to remember to "be spiritual" in a church, at a monastery, or on a mountaintop. It is more difficult to do so when there is an irate customer on the line, your boss wants a report due last week, your teenager just banged up the car, and you have to fire someone that day.

Spirituality is supposed to help us remember to be spiritual, but what does that really mean? One thing that all religious traditions have in common is that the goal of the spiritual life is to raise awareness of a reality that is present to every person in every circumstance. So the Buddhists say, "Before I was enlightened, I chopped wood and carried water. After I was enlightened, I chopped wood and carried water." And thirteenth-century monk Brother Lawrence wrote in *The Practice of the Presence of God:* "When I am in my kitchen, with everyone coming at me from every side, I am just as much in the presence of God as when I am at the altar, ready to take communion."

The key to all spirituality is remembering to be spiritual. We do this by designing practices (some call them disciplines or pieties) that remind us of what we are trying to accomplish. So if we find God in silence, solitude, and simplicity, then we try to create practices or disciplines that will recreate that experience. And if we get really good at it, then we try to teach others to do the same.

Likewise, if we wish to find God in the midst of our daily work lives, then we can devise practices and disciplines to raise our awareness of the divine presence in the midst of the noise, crowds, and complexities of our workplaces. If we do so, then the spirituality of work will help us remember to be spiritual—even on our best days and worst days, even on jobs or tasks we love or on those we cannot stand and wish we did not have to do. And if we get really good at it, then we may even try to teach others to do the same.

A Story about Spirituality

The young monk went to a spiritual master to seek enlightenment: "Show me, Master, how I can find God in my daily tasks of chopping wood and carrying water."

"Chop wood as if it were the most important job in the world," the Master says. "Carry water as if your very life depended on it. Chop wood and carry water so that people say, 'There goes the greatest wood chopper and water carrier of all time.'"

"I do this," the young monk says to the Master, "but still I do not see God."

"You need only look into the wood chips as they fly and into the water as it drips from your bucket," says the Master.

Questions for Reflection and Discussion

....

1. Trying to define spirituality is like trying to nail Jell-O to a tree. Still, write down your own definition of spirituality. Now look at it. Does it necessitate your getting away from the world to practice it? If it does, then rewrite it until you can practice it in the midst of your daily work on your job, with your family, and in your community.

2. Describe one book, movie, television show, or comic strip that you feel gives an accurate depiction of spirituality. Explain why.

3. Describe in detail how you "remember to be spiritual." Are those same techniques successful when you are busy, distracted, or tense? Why or why not?

fifteen

··

A Spirituality for the
Sending Forth

···

WHEN WE TOOK our three teenagers to New York City for the first time a couple of years ago, we found ourselves on the corner of Seventh Avenue and Fifty-sixth Street. "How do you get to Carnegie Hall?" I asked them for probably the hundredth time. "Practice, practice, practice," they groaned in unison at the old joke.

"Actually," I said, "just walk north one block, turn right, and you'll be right there."

Yes, we have to practice our spirituality if we are going to raise our awareness of the presence of God in our workplace and allow that awareness to change how we do our work, but sometimes we are just around the corner from Carnegie Hall and we don't even know it.

The spirituality of work is almost too easy to practice. All it takes is a little creativity and a little discipline. We just have to take things we are already doing at work and turn them into practices (or "disciplines") that remind us to be spiritual in the midst of the hustle and bustle of our daily work (whether that work is paid or unpaid; underpaid, overpaid or justly paid; pleasant or unpleasant; meaningful or not).

These little practices need not be overtly religious. In fact, in most workplaces it is probably better that they are not. The spirituality of work is not about showing off how pious or holy we are. That approach is usually self-defeating. Instead, we need some practices—little reminders, really, that we need to look for the divine presence as we go about our daily work. We need to remember to *be spiritual.*

. . .

These practices or disciplines don't have to be difficult. Work is already hard enough for most of us to lay any degree of asceticism on top of it. The practices we need should be easy. In fact, most of them should be things we are already doing. We just need to turn them into reminders to do what we already want to do anyway—to pay attention to what we are doing, why we are doing it, and how we are doing it.

It might be something as simple as a bell ringing or a computer beeping. It might be something that happens every day or every week or two—like the mail delivery or receiving a paycheck. Whenever these things happen, we need to allow them to help us be spiritual. The trick is asking yourself, "What do I want this occurrence to remind me of?" and answering, "Oh, yeah, I want to notice that God is present in my workplace."

For example, your spiritual discipline might include remembering the birthdays of everyone in your workplace and organizing the signing of a greeting card and baking or buying a birthday cake to celebrate. All you need to do is allow that practice to make you aware that God is, indeed, present in your coworkers and that each one is a "child of

God." Get it? Birthday = child of God = God is present. It's not that difficult.

"I already do a lot of stuff like that," you might say, and I will answer, "Cool, then you are almost to Carnegie Hall." All you have to do now is make these practices into spiritual disciplines. That is, you have to be more intentional about why you are doing these things: When the postman arrives or the paycheck is handed out or the candles are lit on the cake, they have to trigger in you the spiritual response, "God is present; I'd better pay attention to what I'm doing."

. . .

There is a catch, of course. There always is in the spiritual life. You have to practice these disciplines without offending or disturbing others and without disrupting the flow of the work itself.

It is fairly obvious why these precautions are necessary. Most of us work in a pluralistic environment, at least spiritually speaking. We cannot impose our spirituality, much less religion, on our fellow workers. The spirituality of work is not about saying "Praise the Lord" or *"De Colores"* every time something good happens in the workplace. It is about doing the best work of which we are capable in a way that ultimately gives glory to God. The work itself is holy and needs to be done, and our good work is what will show people that we are being spiritual at work, not our overt displays of religiosity.

. . .

Here is one practice that works for me in my workplace, offered more as an example than a suggestion. What is most useful is to develop disciplines that fit your own work environment and flow directly from the work you do.

I am a book publisher and co-owner of my own small publishing house. We publish books on spirituality and religion, as well as books on sports. We have a small staff and I work about five minutes from my home. My spirituality of work flows from my specific work situation.

One of the practices I follow is that when a new book comes in from the printer, I stop whatever I am doing, go to the warehouse, and open a box of the new books. I take one out reverently and check to make sure that everything is fine with it. (You are never really sure what a book will look like until you hold the finished product in your hands.) Then I flip through the book, admiring the beauty of it, smelling the "new book" smell, reading a few passages. Then I think about all the work that went into making the book: the work of the author, the editors, the designers, the typesetters, the printers. I think about all the people who will put more work into the book: the marketers, the booksellers, the customer relations people, the warehouse and fulfillment staff, the truckers and UPS drivers and postal workers, the reviewers. I think about the people who will read this book and how it might give them pleasure or help in some way. Finally, I take five copies of the book, put them in a next-day-air package, and send them to the author, along with a handwritten note of congratulations.

All of this takes five, maybe ten minutes. It does not disrupt the flow of my work or the work of others. It does not disturb or offend others. In fact, I doubt that my staff even realizes what I am doing. Some might call this a prayer, and I would not disagree with them, although it is certainly not the kind of formal prayer I learned when I was younger. But this practice—which occurs only about fifteen to twenty times a year—clearly reminds me that what I do and how I do it is part of God's ongoing creation of the universe and that many others are engaged with me in this work. I then return to work, recharged, restored, and more aware that God is present in my work at all times. This awareness changes how I do my work. It makes me more creative, more competent, more compassionate, and more balanced.

By the way, I practice this discipline whether the book is a title in our religion and spirituality line or one in our line of sports books. It is the book itself and my approach to producing it that makes the work spiritual, not the content. What would be an equivalent practice for you in the work that you do?

A Story about Practicing the Spirituality of Work
....

The CEO was having one of his worst days at work. The board of directors was on his case about cutting costs, there was a new union contract being negotiated, one of his competitors had just lowered its prices, and he had just been contacted by a headhunter about whether or not he'd be interested in moving to a new company.

What's more, things weren't going well at home. His wife hated her job, their kids were acting out in school, and they were having trouble finding good childcare for their youngest child.

Plus, he had been asked to run for city council by a bunch of friends, and they were pressing him for an answer.

So he called his new secretary into his office and asked her how she was doing.

Questions for Reflection and Discussion

....

1. How do you remember to "be spiritual"? When and where do you do it? What little tricks help you, especially in the midst of your daily work?

2. Honestly, which do you care more about: people noticing you or people noticing your work? Why? What do you want them to notice about you? What do you want them to notice about your work?

3. How do you react to people who are overtly religious at work? If you like it, what do you like about it? If you don't like it, what don't you like about it? How do you want to relate to others about your own spiritual life and religious beliefs and practices?

conclusion

I'D LOVE FOR this book to be longer, more complex, more theological, more erudite, but I can't make it so. To me, the spiritual path laid out here is obvious and simple and rewarding and sustainable. It is enough—what a beautiful word. If others want to make spirituality more difficult, they are welcome to try. But for me, this spiritual path is enough. It is enough in the sense that I have already done enough. And it is enough in the sense that I will never have done enough. Both at the same time and at all times.

What I love most about being a Catholic is the Mass. I must have been to more than three thousand of them in my life-time, which means that I have been sent forth that many times to help carry out the mission of Jesus of Nazareth to make this world a better place. Sometimes I have been aware of that sending forth; too many times I have not. When I am aware of the Mass as a sending forth, I realize how powerful it is.

Stick close to the Mass. Do not let anyone or anything dis-tract you from what it really is. Allow it to forgive you, to prepare you, and to send you forth. Leave the church as if you had been shot out of a cannon, embrace your mission to make this a better world, and develop your own spirituality of work to sustain you.

Go in peace to love and serve the Lord.

Thanks be to God.

acknowledgments

FRANK CUNNINGHAM OF Ave Maria Press convinced me to write this book, and Tom Grady and Peter Gehred and Bob Hamma helped me focus and complete it. Thanks to the entire staff at Ave Maria for all your good work.

As always, I have to thank my wife, Kathy. Not only does she support, encourage, and put up with me, but our conversations help me discover what I really believe.

My three children are my constant foils. I'm sure they are sick of all the books and articles I shove their way. Little do they know that they are the ones who have made religion and spirituality real for me.

My colleagues at ACTA Publications allow me to test my ideas about spirituality in the workplace in the real world, and they have taught me more than they will ever know about the kingdom of God.

I also have to thank Bill Droel. Through his efforts with the National Center for the Laity for more than twenty-five years, he has kept alive the idea that the laity's work is primarily in and to the world and that our work is holy.

Finally, thanks to Mom and Dad, married for more than sixty years. They were the ones who baptized me as a Catholic and introduced me to the Mass and convinced me I have a mission that is worthy of my life.

appendix one:

"The Litany of Work"

I RAN ACROSS this litany by David and Angela Kaufmann years ago and had the privilege of publishing it. It is still the best prayer I have ever discovered on the spirituality of work.

> We give thanks, O God, for the work of our lives. *We praise you, God.*
> For the work of our hands, *We praise you, God.*
> For the work of our minds, *We praise you, God.*
> For the work of our hearts, *We praise you, God.*
>
> Response to all: *We praise you, God.*
>
> For the enlightening work of teachers, librarians, students, and coaches,
> For the healing work of doctors, nurses, and counselors,
> For the creative work of artists, musicians, painters, and sculptors,
> For the precise work of engineers, scientists, and computer specialists,
> For the nurturing work of homemakers, parents, and guardians,
> For the wise work of retirees and grandparents,
> For the proclaiming work of writers, photographers, editors, and publishers,
> For the trustworthy work of accountants, bankers, lawyers, politicians, and salespeople,
> For the faith-filled work of ordained, religious, and lay ministers,
> For the protective work of police, firefighters, and military personnel,
> For the dedicated work of secretaries, receptionists, and bookkeepers,
> For the compassionate work of volunteers,
> For the judicious work of managers, administrators, directors, and supervisors,
> For the fruitful work of farmers, fishers, growers, and gardeners,
> For the steadfast work of those who manufacture things,

For the constructive work of builders, surveyors, architects,
    masons, and carpenters,
For the efficient work of those who transport people and things by
    bus, train, plane, taxi, truck, and boat,
For the clarifying work of television, radio, and news media
    workers,
For the dependable work of telephone and postal workers,
For the good work of all other workers,

For our work that sheds light on the darkness, *We praise you, God.*

For our work that creates order from chaos, *We praise you, God.*
For our work that builds peace out of hostility, *We praise you, God.*
For our work that helps others, *We praise you, God.*
For our work that serves others, *We praise you, God.*
For our work that empowers others, *We praise you, God.*
For our work that inspires others, *We praise you, God.*
For our work that enriches and ennobles all creation, *We praise
    you, God.*

appendix two:

A Eucharistic Prayer

AT MY DAUGHTER'S baccalaureate Mass when she graduated
from high school, the priest used a Eucharistic Prayer that I had
never heard before. It fit perfectly the idea of the Mass as a sending
forth. When I asked the priest later which Eucharistic Prayer it was, he
sheepishly admitted that it was not "approved" and asked me not to sic
the "liturgical police" on him. It turned out to be one written by theologian Edward Schillebeeckx at the end of his book, *Christ: The Experience
of Jesus as Lord.* It is presented here with permission of the publisher:

Lord our God,
gathered here around you,
we remember the old story
which has been told down the ages,
of Jesus of Nazareth,
a man who boldly dared to say to you, Lord God,
Abba, Father,
and has taught us to do the same thing.

O God, our Father,
we thank you for this man,
who has changed the face of the earth,
because he spoke of a great vision,
of the kingdom of God which will come one day,
a kingdom of freedom, love, and peace,
your kingdom, the perfection of your creation.

We remember that
wherever your Jesus came,
men rediscovered their humanity,
and so were filled with new riches,
so that they could give one another
new courage in their lives.

We remember
how he spoke to people
about a lost coin,
a sheep that had strayed, a lost son;
of all those who are lost and no longer count,
out of sight, out of mind; the weak and the poor,
all those who are captive, unknown, unloved.

We recall that
he went to search for all who were lost,
for those who were saddened and out in the cold,
and how he always took their side,
without forgetting the others.

And that cost him his life,
because the might of the earth would not tolerate it.
And yet, good God, almighty Father,
he knew that he was understood and accepted by you,
he saw himself conformed by you in love.

So he became one with you.
And so, freed from himself,
he could live a life of liberation for others.

And we remember
how he, who loved us so much
and was one with you, his good Father,
in the last night of his life on earth,
took bread in his holy hands,
blessed, broke, and shared it
at table with his friends, saying:
"This is my body for you."

And what he did filled his heart:
he also took the cup at the table,
gave thanks, praised you, Father, and said:
"Drink this cup, all of you, with me,
for this is my loving covenant with you,
my blood which is shed for reconciliation,
the cup of liberation and happiness."

So when we eat this bread together
and drink this cup,
we do it in remembrance of him, your Son
who is the servant and liberator of us all,
now and ever and beyond death.

Therefore we now also think of the many
who have gone from us, all the people
whom we have loved so much. . . .
Our Father, we cannot believe
that all that they
have meant for us
will now be lost forever.
You are their life, now and always.

We think, too, of the world,
of all who love us in life.
Even the powerful, who have in their hands
the destiny of men, often without knowing them,
the rulers of the world and the church.
Help them and us, so that we may make this earth
a better home for us all;

so that we may make peace and be one
as you, Father, are in your Son,
and he is in you.

So send your Spirit upon us
and upon these gifts, the good Spirit
from you and your Son, that it may inspire us
when we continue to follow Jesus:
Jesus, from whom we have learnt to be free:
free from powers which estrange us,
free to do good.

As best we could, we have done
what Jesus, your witness, who knows our hearts,
commanded us to do:
to celebrate his memory.

In praise and thanks to you,
almighty Father,
in the unity of the Holy Spirit
now too we may and dare
through him and with him and in him
to pray together as he has taught us:
Our Father. . . .

appendix three:

Some Books on the
Spirituality of Work

HERE IS ANOTHER eclectic and personal list. If you want a comprehensive list of books and articles on the spirituality of work, you can look at Peter Hammond's book *Marketplace Bibliography*, or you can visit one of the many websites now devoted to faith and work.

What I am trying to do here is reflect on some particular books that have influenced my understanding of the spirituality of work. There are many other books and authors I admire, but I won't name them here because I don't want to forget to mention some of them. The important thing is not what I read anyhow. It is what you read and what you are looking for that really matters.

The Active Life, by Parker Palmer

I remember that when I first read this book I felt liberated. Here was someone who was saying something about spirituality that I had always felt but was never able to put into words. Palmer feels that spirituality for the active life must be different from that of those in contemplative life. This is so obvious that it shouldn't even need saying, but the thought had never really occurred to me until I read his book. From there, it is just a small step to the spirituality of work.

How to Read a Book, by Mortimer Adler

I remember when one of my teachers assigned this book to us in high school. My parents and siblings all made fun of it: "Greg has to read a book about reading a book." But I read it and used what it said to develop my own way of reading a book, and today I am a writer, editor, and publisher. What I learned from Adler is that reading a book is work—not work in the "Oh, no, I've got to read a book" sort of way, but in the spirituality-of-work sort of way. That is, reading a book has to be done with awareness and attention, just like all our other work.

The Practice of the Presence of God, by Brother Lawrence

I am not big on devotional writing. I've never been able to get into the mystics. But The Practice of the Presence of God, by a simple monk in the middle ages, really struck me. Brother Lawrence was the cook in the monastery kitchen. He probably wasn't educated, and he certainly had no leadership role at the monastery. But Lawrence was holy enough for some people to seek his spiritual advice and write it down, so that today we have this slim volume. What amazed me most about it was the idea that Lawrence could be aware of God's presence in the midst of the "noise and clatter" of his kitchen, with "people coming at me from every side." His inspiration was one of the things that led me to investigate the spirituality of work in my own life.

Crossing the Unknown Sea: Work as a Pilgrimage of Identity, by David Whyte, and Love and Profit: The Art of Caring Leadership, by James Autrey

How can a poet be a consultant to businesses? You can if you're David Whyte. His book *Crossing the Unknown Sea* opened my eyes to the barriers to my imagination I allow to exist, even though they are not really there. Another book like this that has influenced me is *Love and Profit* by James Autry, the former CEO of the Meredith Corporation. Autry is a poet and a successful businessman. I didn't know you could do both until I read his book. His poem on having to fire someone is one of the most painful things I have ever read.

Jesus and His Message: An Introduction to the Good News, by Leo Mahon

I encouraged, edited, and published this book by my pastor emeritus, Father Leo Mahon. It forced me to think a lot about what Jesus was really all about and what he wanted from and for us. I guess I had always believed the "kingdom of God" theology, but Mahon's book crystallized it for me: helping to make this world into a place more like God would have it *is* the mission of every single Christian, whether we realize it or not. It is also a mission that we share with people of good will of all faiths and philosophies, whether *they* realize it or not.

The Measure of All Things: The Seven-Year Odyssey and Hidden Error that Transformed the World, by Ken Alder

I'll let this book stand in for a lot of books like it that have influenced my understanding of the spirituality of work. I like to read books about how people in specific professions do their work. This one is about how two French astronomers, Pierre-Francois-Andre Mechain and Jean-Baptiste-Joseph Delambre, conducted one of history's greatest scientific quests, a mission to measure the Earth and define the meter for all nations and for all time. Two things struck me about their story. First is the meticulousness with which the two scientists went about their work. Second was the fact that their work was still imperfect. In fact, it was wrong, in the sense that the meter was supposed to be one ten-millionth of the distance between the North Pole and the equator, but because of an error it is not—even to this day—exact. Their quest succeeded, even as it failed, and the same can be said of most of our work.

Zen and the Art of Motorcycle Maintenance: An Inquiry into Values,
by Robert M. Pirsig

What I like most about Pirsig's book are the details about caring
for a motorcycle (something I have never done myself). "Working on
a motorcycle, working well, caring, is to become part of the process, to
achieve an inner peace of mind," he writes. I remember thinking when
I read the book: What if all work could be that way? I also liked the way
Pirsig was able to relate the work of daily life with the bigger questions
of science, religion, and values: "The real cycle you're working on is a
cycle called 'yourself.'"

Teaching a Stone to Talk: Expeditions and Encounters, by Annie Dil-
lard, and *Basin and Range,* by John McPhee

These two books are together in my mind because they opened it to
looking closely at the natural world around us. I am kind of an oblivi-
ous guy, and these two books, among others, taught me to look more
carefully at everything around me. Once I started doing that, it was
much easier to experience the presence of God in my work. Besides,
both of these two authors are such good writers of non-fiction that I
hope at least a little of their talent has rubbed off on my own writing.

Anything and everything by John Shea or Alice Camille

John Shea is my personal theologian. I have read almost everything
he has written and have edited and published all of his audio and video
tapes and a couple of his books of stories. What Shea did for me is allow
me to look again at the scriptures and the entire Christian story with
new eyes—the eyes of a storyteller. As I did that, I gained a new understanding of and enthusiasm for my mission in life and the connection
between that mission and my daily work. Another writer who has
helped me understand Catholicism and the scriptures is Alice Camille,
who has written several books for my publishing house, including *Invitation to Catholicism* and *Invitation to the Old Testament* and *Invitation to
the New Testament.*

The Bible, by God and various humans

Once I understood that the Bible is a compelling story about how
we are to live, it became my favorite book of all time. One of the things
that helped this was my volunteering to teach high school religious

education at my parish. I realized very quickly that you cannot lie to teenagers about religion and spirituality, and that if you don't believe what you are teaching yourself, you'd better get out and let someone else do it.

appendix four:
Some Movies on the Spirituality of Work

THIS IS OBVIOUSLY another very eclectic, personal list. It probably also shows my age (fifty-eight). In fact, I own most of these movies on VHS tape rather than DVD, but they are all still available on the Internet. Besides, the point of this list is not to have you run out and watch these particular movies (although there are worse ways to spend a few hours).

What I am trying to show is that if you look carefully at some films (and even at television shows in some cases), you can observe the spirituality of work being practiced. One of the things you will notice is that truly spiritual work is not about how pious the person is but about how and why he or she does the actual work.

It's a Wonderful Life, written by Philip Van Doren Stern and directed by Frank Capra

Most people think of this as a Christmas movie, but I have always thought of it as being about the spirituality of work. What made Jimmy Stewart's character, George Bailey, so appealing and his life so meaningful? It was the way he did his work as a savings and loan executive, community volunteer, husband and father. It was always interesting to me that even though there is an angel in the picture, there is very little depiction of George Bailey's religious life. It is his work that was holy.

A Christmas Carol, written by Charles Dickens and directed by Brian Desmond Hurst

My favorite film version of this classic story is the one starring Alastair Sim. (The ones with George C. Scott and with Michael Caine and the Muppets are also very good.) Much like *It's a Wonderful Life*, this classic tale by Dickens is viewed by most people as a Christmas story, which it certainly is. But it can also be seen as a story of spiritual redemption that can come when we get our work aligned with our deepest and truest values. Remember, it was his work that almost destroyed Ebenezer Scrooge, and once he had his conversion, it was his work that allowed him to help other people, such as the poor, the Cratchit family, and his nephew.

To Kill a Mockingbird, written by Harper Lee and directed by Robert Mulligan

Atticus Finch, the lawyer played by Gregory Peck, is every thinking man's role model as a father. But he was also a competent and fearless lawyer. It was not just the way he tried the case in the movie, it was the way he dealt with his client and his client's family, how he protected his own family, and the gentleness with which he dealt with Boo Radley that demonstrated the spirituality of his work. Again, there is not a lot of religion or piety portrayed in this movie. Much like George Bailey, Atticus Finch was a holy man because of the way he did his work.

Parenthood, written by Lowell Ganz and Babaloo Mandel and directed by Ron Howard

Another movie that depicts the spiritual work of parenting, albeit in very funny terms, is *Parenthood*. Steve Martin plays a business executive who cannot get ahead in his firm because he is trying to balance his work and family life. Jason Robards plays Martin's father, a gruff older man who realizes that the obligations of parenting are never over, no matter how old your kids are. The scenes between Martin and his wife, played by Mary Steenbergen, are funny and excruciatingly painful at the same time.

Mac, written and directed by John Tuturro

Another movie about family and work is the little-known movie, *Mac*. John Tuturro stars as one of three brothers who start their own business building homes. What I like especially are the scenes of the care and quality the brothers put into the homes they build and how proud they are of their work. The opening scene is a beautiful cinematic homage to blue collar work, and Tuturro dedicated the movie to his own father, who apparently was a skilled craftsman.

Norma Rae, written by Irving Raetch and Harriet Frank, Jr., and directed by Martin Ritt

This is another great movie about blue-collar workers. Sally Field won an academy award as best actress for her portrayal of Norma Rae, a Southern textile worker who joins and eventually becomes a leader in a labor union. Ron Liebman plays a union organizer who goes about his work with courage and integrity, always putting the best interests of the workers ahead of his own agenda. Again, there is little mention of organized religion in Norma Rae's life. It is in her work as a mill worker and a union leader, as well as a wife and mother and daughter, that her spirituality lies.

Dead Poet's Society, written by Tom Schulman and directed by Peter Wier

Robin Williams plays John Keating, an iconoclastic and charismatic English professor who inspires his students to live life to the fullest. The scenes of Williams teaching his students to love poetry is a great example of the spirituality of work in action. "What will your contribution be?" he asks his students about the meaning of their life's work. Williams' interactions with his stuffy, inflexible teaching colleagues is also worth viewing.

Patch Adams, written by Patch Adams and Maureen Mylander and directed by Tom Shadyac

Here is Robin Williams again, this time playing Dr. Hunter "Patch" Adams, a real-life doctor. (In my opinion, Williams has a knack for realistically and insightfully portraying people in different occupations as well as anyone.) Again, Williams' character is an iconoclast who is trying to deal with the medical establishment without losing his soul. This movie offers an example of someone who cannot function inside "the system" and must go out and create an alternative way to do his work.

Saving Grace, written by Celia Gittelson and directed by Robert M. Young

OK, I had to have at least one movie about a pope on this list, but this is actually a great movie about the spirituality of work. Tom Conti plays a fictional pope who somehow gets locked out of the Vatican and ends up in a small mountain town in Italy, where nobody recognizes him. The spirit of the townspeople is low, because they are poor and have lost faith in their ability to improve their lives, symbolized by their failure to finish building a new aqueduct to bring water to their town. Conti's character begins rebuilding the aqueduct on his own, eventually joined by the children and widows and eventually the rest of the townspeople. It is the work itself that saves the town's—and the pope's—soul.

The Gospel According to Vic, written and directed by Charles Gormley

Again Tom Conti stars, this time as a teacher in a Catholic school in Scotland. The school is named after "Blessed Edith Semple," a local woman who has been declared "blessed" by the church but needs one more miracle in order to be canonized. Conti works very hard with one particular student who is severely learning handicapped and has a major breakthrough. The student starts functioning normally, and everyone says that it is the miracle the church had been looking for. Conti spends the rest of the movie defending the profession of teaching, insisting it was his good work as a teacher that had cured the boy, not the intervention of a saint. To me, this movie raises a lot of issues about the meaning and holiness of all of our work.

GREGORY F. AUGUSTINE PIERCE, president and co-publisher of ACTA Publications, is the author or editor of ten books, including *Spirituality at Work: 10 Ways to Balance Your Life on the Job*, which has sold over 20,000 copies and won two awards from the Catholic Press Association. He is a former president of the National Center for the Laity, a founder of Business Executives for Economic Justice, and a leader in United Power for Action and Justice. Pierce is a popular national speaker using his sense of humor regarding his own spiritual journey to delight and inspire audiences.

Pierce graduated first in his class at Maryknoll College in 1969 and is the 2000 recipient of the Hillenbrand Award from the Archdiocese of Chicago. Pierce resides in Chicago, Illinois with his wife, Kathy. They are the parents of three college students.

Other Titles of Interest

Sacred Space
The Prayer Book 2008
Jesuit Communication Centre, Ireland

A prayer guide inspired by the popular website, www.sacredspace.ie., this book offers a daily scripture selection followed by points of inspiration to help you consider the passage and its relevance to daily life. Begins at Advent and goes throughout the liturgical year.
ISBN: 9781594711381/ 384 pages / $14.95

Also Available:
Sacred Space for Advent and the Christmas Season
& *Sacred Space for Lent*
visit www.avemariapress.com for details

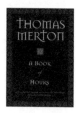

Chasing Joy
Musings on Life in a Bittersweet World
Edward Hays

Edward Hays, a spiritual guide for thousands of spiritual seekers of all faiths around the globe, challenges readers to dig through life's miseries and darkest pains to discover the goodness God continues to promise. Hays uses common joys and struggles of ordinary lives, blending them with some of the great wisdom and traditions of our world to lead readers on the chase to discovering joyful living as God intended.
ISBN: 9780939516780 / 192 pages / $12.95

A Book of Hours
Thomas Merton
Edited by Kathleen Deignan
Foreword by James Finley

The voluminous writings of Thomas Merton have been mined and arranged for the first time into prayers for Dawn, Day, Dusk, and Dark for each of the days of the week. *A Book of Hours* allows readers a slice of monastic contemplation in the midst of their hectic modern life, with psalms, prayers, readings, and reflections.
ISBN: 9781933495057 / 224 pages / $18.95

Available from your bookstore or from
ave maria press / Notre Dame, IN 46556
www.avemariapress.com / Ph: 800-282-1865
A Ministry of the Indiana Province of Holy Cross

Keycode: FØAØ8Ø7ØØØØ